AI-Enabled Analytics for Business

AI-Enabled Analytics for Business

A Roadmap for Becoming an Analytics Powerhouse

Lawrence S. Maisel
Robert J. Zwerling
Jesper H. Sorensen

WILEY

For general information on our other products and services or for technical
support, please contact our Customer Care Department within the United
States at (800) 762-2974, outside the United States at (317) 572-3993 or fax
(317) 572-4002.

Wiley also publishes its books in a variety of electronic formats. Some content
that appears in print may not be available in electronic formats. For more
information about Wiley products, visit our web site at www.wiley.com.

Library of Congress Cataloging-in-Publication Data is Available:

ISBN 978-111-9736-080 (Hardback)
ISBN 978-111-9736-103 (ePDF)
ISBN 978-111-9736-097 (epub)

Cover Design: Wiley
Cover Image: © DNY59/Getty Images

SKY10031685_113021

Contents

Acknowledgments

We thank Kent Bearden, Jonathan Morgan, and Lisa Tapp for sharing their experiences and helping us learn the ways AI and analytics contribute to improving their operations. With gratitude, we also acknowledge the support and editorial assistance of Sheck Cho and Susan Cerra of Wiley, which enabled us to complete this book.

Introduction

Everywhere you turn, you hear or read about artificial intelligence (AI) and the emerging importance of digital transformation. To be competitive in modern business, decision-making needs to evolve into a more objective, insightful, and unbiased process that is powered by the application of AI-enabled analytics.

We have written *AI-Enabled Analytics for Business: A Roadmap for Becoming an Analytics Powerhouse* for executives to gain a solid understanding of AI and analytics that will give clarity, vision, and voice to integrating them in business processes that will be impactful and increase business performance.

Today, there is more promise than practice in implementing AI and analytics for data-driven decisions. As you will learn, there are twice as many analytics failures than successes, and there are twice as many successes that are abandoned rather than sustained. The good news is that almost all failure can be traced back to executive decisions that are entirely avoidable and easily identified.

Further, AI is not the sole purview of big companies, big data, and big data projects that seek to boil the ocean. The butcher, baker, and candlestick maker can all incorporate AI to increase productivity, reduce workforce, retain higher-skilled talent, and enhance the customer's experience. In fact, AI and analytics are better done incrementally, building on each success to scale the business to become an analytics powerhouse.

Our research, training, consulting, and on-the-ground experiences with AI-enabled analytics have shaped our perspectives, refined our practices, and tested our tactics. We have worked side by side with executives like you, and our empirical results demonstrate the critical factor to success is the executive's mindset to the value of analytics and commitment to allocate the resources to building the Analytics Culture.

This book gives you the Roadmap to implement AI and analytics, which, as you will learn, the executive will make or break. As we will show, failure is a choice; the good news is that it is eminently avoidable, and we have specified the steps for success.

In Part I, we cover the fundamentals of AI and analytics, beginning in Chapter 1 to untangle the many seemingly synonymous terms, partitioning tools that do and do not do analytics, and the ROI of AI. It is essential to know the difference between *analysis*, which is the application of arithmetic on data to yield information, and *analytics*, which is the application of mathematics on data to yield insights. In Chapter 2, we illuminate why analytics is essential in business and share Noble Prize-winning research that recognizes the limitations of human decision-making based on biased intuition and gut feel, and why analytics must be included as the essential unbiased component. Chapter 3 discusses myths and misconceptions regarding the approach to analytics, and Chapter 4 takes you through several applications of AI and analytics across different business functions.

In Part II, we define the Roadmap for how to implement AI-enabled analytics for data-driven decisions and the contributions of executives for becoming an analytics powerhouse. Chapter 5 is the fulcrum of this book and delivers a detailed discussion of analytics as more than a tool—it is a culture with four components: Mindset, People, Processes, and Systems. When these components are aligned, immense value to optimize performance is created, and we delineate in depth how this is accomplished. In Chapter 6, you will learn that executive action determines the successful implementation of the Analytics Culture, and you will see what executive actions are needed. Further, we introduce the Analytics Champion, who supports the executive and delivers the tactical implementation of the Analytics Culture. In Chapter 7, we specify with clarity and simplicity how to implement analytics and show that achieving it is not time-consuming, hard, or expensive—it is a discipline. Chapter 8 links analytics to strategic decisions and debuts the new and innovative Analytics Scorecard, which elevates the traditional and subjective Business Scorecard into a quantitative cause-and-effect delineation of strategies that can drive increased business performance.

In Part III, we present specific use cases that illustrate key themes and confirm our approach and insights conveyed in earlier chapters. As there is more to learn from failure than success, Chapter 9 discusses instances across several industries where analytics successes became failures. Chapter 10 tells the story of a hospitality company's analytics proof of concept that yielded optimized staffing while maintaining excellent customer service, significant cost savings, and opportunities to boost revenue and profit—yet failed because the senior executive did not believe in investing in analytics. Chapter 11 is the story of achieving insights that incrementally progress toward a data-driven culture from analytics in demand planning and supply chain. Finally, Chapter 12 puts an exclamation point on the notion that AI and analytics are for everyone, not just big companies, through the story of a medium-size art museum and its CFO's curiosity, which led to learning about analytics and discovering how it provides insights.

For your convenience, we have also included an appendix for the Analytics Champion that will guide the executive in selecting the right person and provide the Champion with skillsets and tools needed for implementing the first analytics project and scaling the Analytics Culture.

An executive's job is to manage risk, not avoid it. Yet many executives are too risk-averse and choose not to make decisions because the risk of failure blinds them to see the opportunity for success. While information is nearly always imperfect, employing AI and analytics gives vision to the future that mitigates risk for better decision-making. This book is for you, the executive and aspiring executive, to arm you with the knowledge to lead your organization to become an analytics powerhouse.

With this introduction, we welcome you to the Undiscovered Country—the future!

PART
I

Fundamentals

CHAPTER 1

A Primer on AI-Enabled Analytics for Business

*Knowledge will forever govern ignorance; and a
people who mean to be their own governors must arm
themselves with the power which knowledge gives.*

—James Madison[1]

Artificial intelligence (AI) dates back over 75 years. Alan Turing, a mathematician, explored the mathematical possibility of AI, suggesting that "humans use available information as well as reason in order to solve problems and make decisions," and if this premise is true, then machines can do so too. This was the basis of his 1950 paper "Computing Machinery and Intelligence," in which he discussed "how to build intelligent machines and how to test their intelligence."[2]

So, what is artificial intelligence? *Very broadly* speaking, it is the ability of a machine to make decisions that are done by humans. But what does that mean, what does AI look like, and how will it change our lives and society?

We all know that AI, sooner or later, will be part of all businesses. But *when* it is part of the business is entirely dependent on what each executive knows and understands about AI and analytics. And here lies the chasm between the early adopters and the rest of the pack.

According to Grant Thornton's 21 May 2019 report "The Vital Role of the CFO in Digital Transformation," the 2019 CFO Survey of Tech Adoption covered several technologies, including advanced analytics and machine learning. 38% of respondents indicated that they currently implemented advanced analytics, and 29% are planning implementations in the next 12 months. For machine learning technology, the survey results said that 29% had implemented it and 24% were planning to implement in the next 12 months. Impressive returns from the survey's sample set, and indicative of the priority of and accelerating trend in the adoption of analytics and AI throughout business. However, while conveying progress in its best light, this survey is a poor showing of a glass that is not even half full.

Implementations of AI are just scratching the surface, as projects have been highly targeted to only certain areas of the business and for certain tasks. So, while the movement to incorporate advanced analytics is in the right direction, there are many more failures than successes. This is disturbingly bad news, which we shall learn largely rests with executives. The good news is that AI and analytics failures are eminently avoidable.

Many executives lack clarity of vision and voice to how they will navigate their business, division, group, or department through the adoption of analytics and AI. Other executives think they know what AI enablement means but are often working from poorly defined terms or misconceptions about analytics. Their knee-jerk response is to hire consultants and buy AI-enabled analytics software without fully understanding how analytics will be used to drive decisions.

Cries of "We need better forecasting" and "What factors are driving our business?" and "We must get smarter about what we do" echo in boardrooms and executive conference rooms. But how exactly is this done? Not *what*, but *how*? The "what," many an executive has read from a mountain of consulting reports; but the "how" is unclear and is why too many businesses are lagging in their adoption of AI and analytics.

In this chapter, we lay the foundation for this book by untangling terms and terminology with definitions and giving a ground-level introduction in select technologies (for the purpose of understanding, not to become experts). We will pursue a high-level discussion of AI, machine learning (ML), and analysis vs. analytics, followed by an explanation of business intelligence and data visualization and how these are different from analytics. We will introduce the application of AI-enabled analytics in the context of insights and the contrast between biased vs. unbiased predictions. Finally, we will position the importance of AI by discussing its ROI.

AI AND ML—SIMILAR BUT DIFFERENT

We see the widely used phrase "AI and ML" and conjure these as linked at the hip; but while related, they are not one and the same. First, AI is a *superset*, covering all that is considered artificial intelligence. The overarching concept of AI is simply a machine that can make a human decision. Any mode of achieving this human decision by a machine is thus AI, and machine learning is one such mode or *subset* of AI. Therefore, all ML is AI, but not all AI is ML.

Accordingly, ML is *one* form of AI. ML is a widely used method for implementing AI, and there are many tools, languages, and techniques available. ML engages algorithms (mathematical models) that computers use to perform a specific task without explicit instructions, often relying on patterns and inference, instead.

Another popular form of AI is neural networks that are highly advanced and based on mirroring the synapse structure of the brain. So, ML and neural networks are both subsets of AI, as depicted in Figure 1.1, as well as other forms of AI (that is, any other technology/ technique that enables a machine to make a human decision).[3]

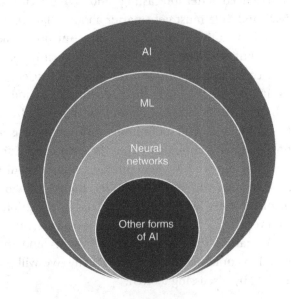

Figure 1.1 Superset and subsets of AI.

MACHINE LEARNING PRIMER

This section offers a brief orientation to ML. ML is a technique and technology that today requires specialized skills to use and deploy. ML is an AI engine often used with other tools to render the ML output useful for decisions. For example, suppose a bank wants to expand the number of loans without increasing the risk profile of its loan portfolio. ML can be used to make predictions regarding risk, and then the results are imported to spreadsheets to report those new additional loan applicants that can now be approved.

Large ML projects often involve the collaboration of data scientists, programmers, database administrators, and application developers (to render a deliverable outcome). Further, ML needs large volumes of high-quality data to "train" the ML model, and it is this data requirement that causes 8 of 10 ML and AI projects to stall.[4] While ML is popular and powerful, it is not easy. Many new software applications are making ML use easier, but it is still mostly for data scientists.

Before an ML project can begin, its "object" must be defined: that is, what is to be solved. For example, suppose we want to predict which customers on our ecommerce website will proceed to check out (vs. those who exit before checking out). As presented in Figure 1.2, the process to go from the object to deployed solution has many steps, including collection of data, preparation of data, selecting the algorithm and its programming, model training, model testing, and deployment. Any failure at any point will require a reset and/or restart back to any previous point in the process.[3]

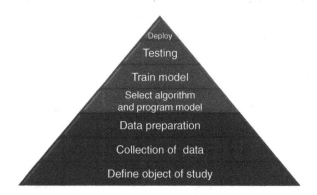

Figure 1.2 ML process.

ML has a limitation in that the solution of the object is highly specific to the data used to train the ML model. Most often, the model is not transportable, even to a similar business or a similar department within the same business. Also, as mentioned, the use of ML often requires other tools to render its results useful for consumption by business managers. However, while complex, ML can offer high business value with a wide range of applications: for example, predicting customer churn, sales deals that will close in the next 60 days, drugs that are likely to proceed to the next phase in trials, customers who are more likely to buy with a 5% discount, demand forecasting, and so on.

ANALYTICS VS. ANALYSIS

Another set of terms to get our arms around is *analysis* and *analytics*. Analysis, in business reporting, involves calculations of arithmetic (add, subtract, multiply, and divide), whereas analytics for business encompasses mathematics (algebra, trigonometry, geometry, calculus, etc.) and statistics (about the study of outcomes).

In a profit and loss statement, there is a variance analysis of current year actual performance against budget. The analysis is expressed as the difference in dollars and as a percent. The variance analysis uses arithmetic to make a measurement of the existing condition of the company compared to what it planned for the year. This analysis is comparative *information* from arithmetic on data and descriptive of a current situation, but it is not an *insight* that is additive to a decision.

Insight, as defined with respect to the value from data, is that *not known about the business and when known should affect decisions*, and insights are derived from analytics that applies mathematics to data.

For example, say sales are down 15% for the past three months, but sales are predicted to increase this month. This prediction is based on a correlation of unemployment as a three-month inverse leading indicator to sales, meaning as unemployment goes down, sales will go up. In this example, unemployment has been dropping for the past three months, so the prediction is for sales to increase in the current month.

The use of correlations to make a prediction is analytics that reveals an insight, which was not known from the data or information from the analysis of the data, and which when known will affect decisions. In this case, without knowing the prediction of the lead indicator, the business would run deep discounts to attract sales. However, knowing that sales are predicted to reverse direction would cause the business not to discount or to only offer small discounts.

As such, to crystalize and distinguish the important definitions of *insights* and *information*, we repeat that *insights* are derived from the application of *mathematics* on data, while *information* is derived from the application of *arithmetic* on data. *Information* is used to *support* a decision, whereas *insights* are used to *affect* a decision.

Accordingly, analytics can powerfully reveal unbiased insights, as it applies mathematics on data that is void of the personal and political pressures that are exerted on humans when they make forecasts and predictions. As humans, we want the future to be what we desire or what we need, so we can make any forecast come to our desired outcome. As such, analytics is especially potent to enable unbiased data-driven decisions.

BI AND DATA VISUALIZATION VS. ANALYTICS

Business intelligence (BI) tools date back to the 1980s and enabled multidimensional reporting. BI went beyond spreadsheets to ingest large amounts of data from several data sources and then segment (into separate dimensions) the data into hierarchies. This approach gave users the ability to organize and dive into more data more intelligently.

Today, legacy BI tools have essentially become data-marts for data extraction into spreadsheets for reporting. BI tools are largely maintained by IT and require programming to build *cubes* (specialized BI databases) to respond to predefined questions. However, legacy BI is too rigid and complex for most users, so IT departments often program user-requested reports and data extractions (for download to other applications).

The complexity of BI gave birth to data visualization tools that were introduced in the 2000s and offered graphic representations of data in many forms, often combined into *dashboards* to render a story about key aspects of the business. Dashboards can be informative but typically not analytical.

The reference to data visualization says it all in its name. It is *visualizing* data, not applying mathematics on data. An excerpt from a 2019 report from the Finance Analytics Institute (www.fainstitute.com), "Visualization vs. Analytics, what each tool is, how they are different & where they apply," offers a clear discussion of visualization:[4]

Dashboards are of prime value to combine visual charts with tabular data of KPIs and key values for comparisons.

The picture below is . . . where data and images of trends can work together to offer a view to the past and present. Like a car's dashboard, the numerical readings at the top tell key performance data needed to be known; e.g. if we're running low on gas. . .

But dashboards are not predictive, and views of past data can lead to false negatives or positives of the future. Look at the image below [Figure A]. . .

The historical trend is essentially up. So, what's the next bar to follow? Up? Down? What decision would you make if you predicted up? What would happen if you guessed wrong? As seen on the chart below [Figure B], the next bar was substantially down.

Figure A

Figure B

Visualization gives colors and images that intrigue the eye. But there is pretty and there is practical, and the two should not be confused—although they often are. Far too frequently, dashboards become an exercise in art vs. business. The rendering of a dashboard should be to make better decisions; so when viewing a dashboard, always ask, "Will what I'm seeing help inform me to make a better decision? What decision?" If the answer is not definitive, then the dashboard is art, not business.

We like to say that AI and analytics can *torture data until it confesses!* The "confession" obtained from analytics, which applies mathematics on data, can better inform us about the future; and decisions are about the future! Consider, have you ever made a decision about the past? Well, no, other than to say that the decision you made when the past was the future turned out to be a good or bad decision. While this bit of time travel may be confusing, the point is that using tools that display data from the past is only part of the inputs needed to make decisions about the future.

Therefore, it is important to distinguish that data visualization is largely a tool of reporting and displaying past data and information, whereas AI and analytics tools use past data to bring insights that make predictions and forecasts about the future.

For example, returning to the two charts in Figure A and Figure B, the question was what the next bar would be on the trend in Figure A: up or down? A viewer of the chart might lean to *up* because the general direction of the trend is up or due to a personal need/desire to have the trend continue up. However, applying the statistical process control index on the data in Figure A would predict the next bar to be materially down—which it was, as depicted in Figure B.

This is a beautiful example of applied statistics to reveal an unbiased insight that can, and should, materially impact a decision. Whereas reporting and data visualization informs what happened and where it happened, analytics powerfully advises what will happen and how to make it happen. As we shall explore in depth in Chapter 5, using the full range of tools, decisions can be enhanced through information and insights that span a continuum of time in the past, present, and future.

BIASED VS. UNBIASED

Most planning, budgeting, and forecasting are *biased:* that is, a value for the future that is based on a human's guess. While the guess may be from experience or gut feel, it is a value that is not mathematically calculated from past performance of the business. Biased forecasts are always fraught with human frailties because, as mentioned, they are about what we want or need the future to be. How many times have you made a spreadsheet and not liked the outcome displayed? Hardly ever, for most of us—we simply change the values and, voilà, get what we want. Biased decision-making will be explored further in Chapter 2.

Many sales teams pronounce their "forecasts" with immense certitude by claiming the forecast is from the CRM system. The importance of the CRM is to establish the credentials of the source, like the Good Housekeeping seal of approval. It is authority, credibility, and accuracy all rolled into one. But—and this is a big *but*—the forecast is merely the sales rep's guess of when the deal will close.

A company typically establishes a ranking system for where a sales deal is in the pipeline and its probability to close, but as disciplined as this ranking may be, it is not "analytics"—that is, it is not derived from the application of mathematics on data. The fact the sales rep enters the "forecast" into the CRM does not transform it to anything beyond a guess.

While sales reps are often good guessers, they achieve many of their forecasts, especially at the end of a quarter, through a modicum of "unnatural" acts that have deep discounts and concessions the business pays for in reduced profitability down the road.

Analytics provides unbiased intelligence that is an essential input into decisions, as the mathematics of analytics is dispassionate. Formulas have no predisposition to a desired outcome. Data about the past is historical. As such, the combination of math and history yields a view to what the future can be vs. what one wants the future to be.

Business needs human intuition, as we have a good sense of what is around us, but *we are biased about what is ahead of us*. As such, when looking forward, there is a fundamental need to incorporate unbiased predictions and forecasts that can be gained from analytics. When the two are combined, the man-and-machine efforts produce higher accuracy predictions over a longer time horizon.

AI AND ROI

Research typically pegs the ROI on analytics at a minimum of 10X. For example, according to Boston-based NUCLEUS Research, the 2014 survey on Analytics ROI revealed that the average return "has increased to $13.01 for every Analytics dollar invested."[5] An excerpt from a November 2011 Research Note from NUCLEUS Research highlights the visibility that analytics provides:[6]

> Software buyers may think that vendors overhype visibility as a benefit of analytics, but Nucleus found that, in fact, the highest-ROI analytics deployments made data more available to decision makers and enabled them to find ways to increase revenues or reduce costs. Nucleus found analytics enabled improved visibility in three areas:
> - Revenues. The more managers knew about what customers where (sic) buying and why, the better able they were to accelerate sales cycles, cross sell, and maximize pricing.
> - Gross margin. By serving up highly granular data on costs of goods sold, analytics applications helped decision makers identify the highest margin products so that they could push the right products and increase gross profit.

- Expenses. The more managers . . . learned [from] analytics . . . the better able they were to reduce or eliminate expenditures that were unnecessary or generated low returns.

As seen in Figure 1.3, the report "The Analytics Advantage, We're just getting started," from Deloitte, reflects key findings from the Deloitte Analytics Advantage Survey, including "Nearly half of all respondents (49 percent) assert that the greatest benefit of using analytics is that it is a key factor in better decision-making capabilities." Further, when asked "Does analytics improve competitive positioning?" some 55% of respondents indicated that analytics Fairly to Significantly improved positioning.[7]

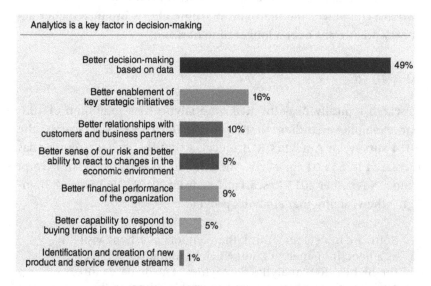

Figure 1.3 Deloitte analytics for decision-making.

With executives agreeing on the value of analytics for decisions and competitive capability, we note that business performance betterment projects must be measurable, and AI is no exception. To this end, we believe that all analytics projects should start with a proof-of-concept or pilot to ensure that the quantification of benefits are measured, material, and achievable.

For example, at a data science conference, many speakers crowed about their projects with AI and analytics. But what was notably absent in most of the presentations was a slide on ROI. In one session, a member of the audience specifically asked about ROI. In a proud fashion, the presenting data scientist said the project saved enough money to hire another data scientist! Self-perpetuation is not ROI, and this example highlights the need to benchmark AI's contribution to business performance.

CONCLUSION

We live in an exciting time for change. Much has been done by business to advance productivity, and with it, people's lives. For example, at the turn of the twentieth century, the invention of electric power and the electric motor fundamentally and dramatically changed society, with immense benefits for mankind. Even more than the electric motor's introduction, AI will make profound changes over the next generation and beyond.

Essentially, all businesses today realize that AI and analytics must be incorporated. Some know what AI-enabled analytics is; but, unfortunately, only a few know how to incorporate AI, and then only on a limited basis. The goal of this book is to empower all leaders with vision and clarity about *how to* implement a *culture* of analytics for data-driven decisions and to provide a Roadmap to get there. In the next chapter, we discuss why AI and analytics need to be part of business, regardless of size.

NOTES

1. BrainyQuote. (n.d.). James Madison quotes. https://www.brainyquote.com/quotes/james_madison_135446.
2. Turin, A.M. (1950). Computing machinery and intelligence. *Mind* 49: 433–460. https://www.csee.umbc.edu/courses/471/papers/turing.pdf.
3. Zwerling, R.J. and Sorensen, J.H. (2019). AI & ML basics in business. Finance Analytics Institute, Analytics Academy.
4. Zwerling, R.J. and Sorensen, J.H. (2019). Visualization vs. analytics, what each tool is, how they are different & where they apply. Finance Analytics Institute, Analytics Academy.

5. McDonald, A. (2015). Analytics ROI—how to measure and maximize the value of analytics? Eckerson Group. https://www.eckerson.com/articles/analytics-roi-how-to-measure-and-maximize-the-value-of-analytics.

6. Nucleus Research. (2011). Analytics pays back $10.66 for every dollar spent. Research Note. https://www.ironsidegroup.com/wp-content/uploads/2012/06/1122-Analytics-pays-back-10.66-for-every-dollar-spent.pdf.

7. Deloitte. (2013). The analytics advantage: we're just getting started. dttl-analytics-analytics-advantage-report-061913.pdf (deloitte.com).

CHAPTER 2

Why AI-Enabled Analytics Is Essential for Business

All models are wrong; some are useful.

—George Box[1]

We are at the dawn of an era of digitization for business that requires on-demand continuous planning where human and artificial intelligence (AI) work hand in hand to achieve insights for better results from data-driven decisions. New software and cloud computing are making analytics more available, but is business adopting these new tools at a break-neck pace? Well, no! The adage "You can lead a horse to water, but can't make him drink" is sadly applicable to many business experiments in analytics that have proven successful—but all too often are not sustained.

We will explore in subsequent chapters the impediments to analytics, but here our attention turns to why analytics is essential for business and why the executive must embrace the implementation of AI and analytics.

First, without analytics, the business cannot remain competitive and will be at risk of making decisions that fail to recognize market opportunities, ineffectively deploy capital, and misallocate staff resources to low-value efforts. Second, without analytics-based decisions, we as humans will continue to be inherently biased, which leads to under-optimized performance. Third, executives pursuing analytics have a better chance of being rewarded from improved business performance; those who do not risk being passed over. Accordingly, we will dive into the competitiveness, decision processes, and career advancement that analytics supports.

COMPETITIVENESS

Today's competitive landscape requires the adoption of analytics for business to remain competitive, growing, and profitable. The business that can plan better, wins! For example, if Company A can more accurately forecast its demand, then it gains efficiency over costs and use of capital to better allocate to grow its markets; whereas Company B, which has failed to better forecast demand, loses market share due to the inability to fulfill demand or inefficiency in its costs that leads to higher prices.

This example seems obvious, yet the stampede to incorporate AI-enabled analytics in business is slow to develop, often from the lack of people skills and analytics tools, but primarily from an executive's perspective to under-value the benefits from AI. Until executives understand and believe in the value from AI, business will confront massive amounts of data with spreadsheets, which is akin to taking a cross-country trip on a tricycle. Fine if you have the time—but you don't.

Unfortunately, too many executives do not appreciate or understand the value of AI and analytics to solve business problems, such as optimizing areas of the business and actions that can be derived from insights to improve the business. This is due to several factors, including lack of executive training on analytics, no advocate emerging to make a compelling case for analytics, and, as is often true with other innovations, executives who are risk-averse about investing in what they do not understand or accepting a risk of failure.

The lessons learned from prior business technology revolutions have taught that the need to enter the modern digital transformation era is a requirement and not an option. In times past, businesses that have not evolved with the changes have perished or, worse, become insignificant players in their industry segment.

Think IBM, once the preeminent and dominant name in computers in the twentieth century, is little spoken of in the 2020s. Still a $70 billion company, IBM is not a point of presence in Silicon Valley, which has bred competitors to take mindshare when it comes to computer innovation and relevance. Think too of Kodak, born in the 1880s, a onetime "blue-chip" company that held 90% of the film and 85% of the camera market in the United States. As late as 1996, it was a $16 billion company with 145,000 employees. But the switch to digital cameras and smartphones decimated Kodak, and by 2012, Kodak filed for bankruptcy protection.[2]

In comparing the 1955 Fortune 500 list of companies to the 2019 list, there remain only 52 companies. The penalty for not recognizing the emerging digital transformation era will be just as severe. Companies like Blackberry, Nokia, and Motorola are shadows of the prevailing players they once were in the market they shaped. Conversely, companies like Amazon and Netflix have led the way and dominated with AI and analytics. Note, though, that adverse consequences are not limited to large companies and are equally applicable to companies of any size or industry, and public, private, profit, or non-profit.

The executive who does not realize the value from analytics or fails to adopt will be replaced by an executive who can deliver insights for data-driven decisions. This is inevitable because executives who fail to do so will endanger their company's performance and competitive position.

HUMAN JUDGMENT AND DECISION-MAKING

In business, human decision-making does not always optimize performance because it is vulnerable to bias and intuition: that is, gut feel. We are naturally intuitive about the future but quantitatively limited to calculate what the future probably can be. We react to events and rely on experience to "guide" us to a decision. We also may have a personal want or need that influences and impacts our decisions.

As such, we must first understand how nature has wired us to make decisions before we can appreciate and accept how analytics can contribute to enhancing decision-making that can lead to improved business performance. The need to balance our instinctive judgment with AI for decisions is necessary to fulfill the potential value of analytics in business and avoid the shortcomings associated with traditional decision-making.

The research of Kahneman and Tversky, who received the Nobel Prize for Economics in 2002, produced a ground-breaking understanding of human judgment and decision-making under uncertainty. Their research is viewed as one of the most influential social science behavioral insights of the past century. It challenged the notion held by many economists that the human mind is unconsciously rational.

Kahneman authored a book, *Thinking, Fast and Slow*; the central thesis is the interplay between what he terms *System 1* and *System 2* thinking.[3] In System 1, a person has an instinctual response that is automatic and rapid and has been shaped by experience and expertise. For example, how much is 2 plus 2? Hopefully, you said 4. Your response was immediate and almost instinctive because, over many years, this simple answer has always been the same. In effect, System

1 seeks coherence and applies relevant memories to explain events or make decisions.

System 2 is invoked for more complex, thoughtful reasoning and is characterized by slower, more rational analysis but is "prone to laziness and fatigue." If you want to conduct your own experiment along these lines, ask someone to write down the results of a hypothetical sequence of 20 coin flips. Then ask the person to flip a coin 20 times and write down the results. The actual flips will almost certainly contain streaks of only heads or tails—the sorts of streaks that people do not think a random coin produces on its own. This kind of misconception leads us to incorrectly analyze all sorts of situations in business, politics, and everyday life.

Further, the research of Kahneman and Tversky revealed previously undiscovered patterns of human irrationality: the ways that our minds consistently fool us and the steps we can take, at least some of the time, to avoid being fooled. They used the word *heuristics* to describe the rules of thumb that often lead people astray.

One such rule is the *halo effect*, in which thinking about one positive attribute of a person or thing causes observers to perceive other strengths that are not actually there. For example, a project team was discussing the status of a new marketing campaign. The campaign was led by Billy, who had a reputation for delivering successful campaigns. Team members were asked to give their assessment of progress and, recognizing Billy's past successes, gave positive evaluations. This reflected the halo effect in that the past successes extended to this project without any factual basis other than Billy's reputation.

This work has led to advances in individual behavior. It is full of practical little ideas like "No one ever made a decision because of a number"; Kahneman has said, "They need a story." Or Tversky's theory of socializing: because stinginess and generosity are both contagious, and because behaving generously makes you happier, surround yourself with generous people.

The research has clarified how decisions are made and underlying influences that can impact decisions. These influences are inherent in group interactions and individual biases, which are key to understanding the balance between human judgment and analytics in decision-making.

Group Decision-Making

Several recognized behavioral group decision-making processes occur in forms that are considered flawed because they contain bias. They lack the tools of analytics to inject unbiased insights into the decision process. One of these occurrences is often referred to as the *Abilene paradox*, where a group of people collectively decide on a course of action that is counter to the preferences of many or all of the individuals in the group.[4] It involves a common breakdown of group communication in which each member mistakenly believes that their own preferences are counter to the group's and, therefore, does not raise objections. A common phrase relating to the Abilene paradox is a desire to "not rock the boat."

For example, the design team of a successful smartphone is deciding whether to remove the home button on its next version release. The lead designer suggests that the home button be kept, and the decision, after some discussion, is to keep the home button. Later that day, some of the design team meet for lunch, and Peter expresses his preference for removing the home button. Mickey jumps in to say "Me too!" and is followed by Davey. They all acquiesced to the decision since they believed they were the only ones who did not agree. In fact, when the team reassembled, most of the other members also preferred to remove the home button but also did not express their preference.

Another group decision-making process is *groupthink*, a mode of thinking in which individual members of small cohesive groups tend to accept a decision that represents a perceived group consensus, whether or not the group members believe it to be valid, correct, or optimal.[5] Groupthink reduces the efficiency of collective problem solving within such groups and perpetuates bias and flawed assumptions.

For example, a capital project review team is convened to decide on next year's CapEx budget. Each member is asked to indicate their preferred #1 project. After the first and second members express their preference for the same project, each succeeding member agrees with the first two, although their individual preferences were different. They "go along to get along" and express their agreement with the preferred project.

Ronald Sims writes that the Abilene paradox is like groupthink but differs in significant ways, including that in groupthink, individuals are not acting contrary to their conscious wishes and generally feel good about the decisions the group has reached.[6] According to Sims, in the Abilene paradox, the individuals acting contrary to their own wishes are more likely to have negative feelings about the outcome. In Sims' view, groupthink is a psychological phenomenon affecting clarity of thought, whereas in the Abilene paradox, thought is unaffected.

These group decision-making processes demonstrate the embedded flaws in human behavior that can produce decisions that lead to under-optimized, inefficient, ineffective, or non-competitive business performance that wastes capital and resources. This punctuates why unbiased, scientific AI and analytics inputs are essential to minimize or eliminate group bias and contribute to improved business performance.

Individual Bias in Decision-Making

Individuals think in System 1 (thinking fast), which is the intuitive, "gut reaction" for making decisions. System 2 (thinking slow) is the analytical, "critical thinking" way of making decisions. Most of us identify with System 2 thinking. We consider ourselves rational, analytical beings. Thus, we believe we spend most of our time engaged in System 2 thinking. Actually, we spend almost all of our decision-making engaged in System 1. Only if we encounter something unexpected, or if we make a conscious effort, do we engage System 2.

System 1 thinking produces various forms of bias; several of the critical modes of bias more recognized by behavioral psychologists are discussed next:

- *Inherent bias:* One of the biggest problems with System 1 is that it seeks to quickly create a coherent, plausible story—an explanation for what is happening—by relying on associations and memories, pattern-matching, and assumptions. The amount and quality of the data on which the story is based are largely irrelevant. System 1 will default to a plausible, convenient story even if that story is based on incorrect information.

For example, suppose a customer who usually orders a certain product places an order for an amount considerably less than expected. Management assumes the customer's business is down, when, in fact, the competitor has captured the customer's business. In effect, management has rationalized the event rather than seeking objective information on the cause.

- *Hindsight bias*: People will reconstruct a story around past events to underestimate the extent to which they were surprised by those future events. This is an "I knew it all along" bias. If an event comes to pass, people exaggerate the probability that they knew it was going to occur. If an event does not occur, people erroneously recall that they thought it was unlikely. In either case, these interpretations were based on subjective (biased) use of data.

  For example, revenue forecasts received from marketing indicated that product sales would grow even though last month's sales were below budget. However, actual sales were materially below the forecast, upon which the executive says, "I knew it all along" in hindsight, but that concern was not acted upon when the forecast was accepted.

- *Confirmation bias:* People will be quick to seize on limited evidence that confirms their existing perspective. And they will ignore or fail to seek evidence that runs contrary to the coherent story they have already created in their mind.

  For example, imagine a business considering launching a new product. The CEO has an idea for the "next big thing" and directs the team to conduct market research. The team launches surveys, focus groups, and competitive analysis. However, to satisfy the CEO, the team seeks to confirm the idea, only accepting evidence to support the feasibility of the product and disregarding contradictory information.

- *Noise bias:* According to Kahneman and Sibony,[7] *noise* is the variability when making judgments that go in *different* directions. For example, a company is building a new plant to manufacture its recently approved flu medicine. The plant is scheduled to be online in six months. The project team was asked to estimate (judge) when the first shipment could be expected, and the estimates ranged from 3 months ahead of schedule to 12 months behind schedule. This variability is the noise in judgment and significantly influences the decisions that follow and the operating impacts affected by these judgments.

These examples illustrate the risks inherent in individual biases that can steer decision-making in the wrong direction. They also demonstrate the need for unbiased AI-enabled analytics input to be a powerful counterbalance to make more effective decisions that improve business performance.

As humans, we cannot avoid our natural instinct that drives us to System 1 thinking for most of our daily lives. It is important for us to recognize when we are relying on it incorrectly for decision-making and the need to force System 2 thinking that incorporates AI and analytics as the preferred way to arrive at important business decisions and actions.

CONCLUSION

The era of human judgment for decision-making needs to evolve into a process that is more objective, insightful, and unbiased. AI-enabled analytics is the vehicle to introduce in the decision process to support or contradict human bias. As such, organizations must adopt an Analytics Culture that values the need for data-driven decisions as essential to assure and improve business performance.

NOTES

1. The actual quote is, "Remember that all models are wrong; the practical question is how wrong do they have to be to not be useful": George E.P. Box. Draper, N.R. (2007). *Response Surfaces, Mixtures, and Ridge Analyses*, 63. John Wiley & Sons.
2. Daniel Kahneman, an Israeli-born psychologist, and Amos Nathan Tversky, an Israeli cognitive and mathematical psychologist, received the Nobel Prize for Economics in 2002 for their integration of psychological research into economic science. Their pioneering work examined human judgment and decision-making under uncertainty and the discovery of systematic human cognitive bias and handling of risk.

3. Kahneman, D. (2011). *Thinking, Fast and Slow*. Farrar, Straus, and Giroux.

4. The term was introduced by Jerry B. Harvey in a 1974 article, "The Abilene Paradox: The Management of Agreement." The name of the phenomenon comes from an anecdote that Harvey uses in the article to elucidate the paradox.

5. Schmidt, A. (2016). Groupthink. In: *Encyclopedia Britannica*. https://www.britannica.com/science/groupthink.

6. Sims, R.R. (1994). *Ethics and Organizational Decision Making: A Call for Renewal*, 55–56. Greenwood Publishing Group.

7. Adapted from Kahneman, D. and Sibony, O. (2021). *Noise: A Flaw in Human Judgment*. Hachette Book Group. As discussed with Kahneman and Sibony in: McKinsey. (2021). Sounding the alarm on system noise. Strategy & Corporate Finance Practice.

CHAPTER 3

Myths and Misconceptions About Analytics

Myths that are believed tend to become true.

I t is natural to accept "common knowledge," particularly when our knowledge of a subject is limited, regardless of whether that knowledge is in fact true. For example, most of us have heard of a 97% consensus among scientists that humans are causing global warming or that inhaling secondhand smoke causes cancer. However, there are many peer-reviewed publications from sources ranging from Houston University to the *Journal of the National Cancer Institute* that dispute these claims, yet most of us have not heard of these contradictory findings.[2,3]

Similarly, there is the need to dispel some common knowledge about implementing AI-enabled analytics. One example is that implementing analytics is complex and expensive. However, as we discuss in detail in the chapters that follow, the Roadmap to AI-enabled analytics is not hard, long, or expensive—it is simply disciplined.

Executives must take heed to avoid the "myths and misconceptions" about an Analytics Culture that include (i) data scientist misconception and myth, (ii) shot in the dark, (iii) bass-ackward, (iv) AI is not IT, (v) big is not better, and (vi) not now. As we will explain, data scientists, consultants, and IT all have roles in AI and analytics; but when implementing an analytic culture, the user is the primary player, with all others playing contributing roles. Too often, the roles are reversed, and the users are secondary.

DATA SCIENTIST MISCONCEPTION AND MYTH

Many businesses assume that implementing analytics requires data scientists, as they have the skills required for AI and know how to apply AI in the business. While the former assumption is true, the latter is a misconception.

With respect to knowledge of business, we note that the typical data scientist is essentially a programmer who knows statistics. Their realm is IT and not business, and the two domains are worlds unto themselves. For example, the following bullet points are an excerpt from a profile on LinkedIn for an IT Director of Digital Process Automation for a major insurance company. While there are lots of technical accolades, there is little discussion of business application or benefits, and no delineation of ROI:

- Managing a global team of 30+ RPA Architects, Programmers, Data Scientists, Technical Business Analysts and onsite consultants from Appian, InfoSys, IBM, and Cognizant
- Managing the implementation of a Business Process Management Tool (Appian) into an on-premises architecture to automate & streamline Client Onboarding
- Integrating InfoSys's ML Platform (NIA) and continuing to release new stories in 6-week intervals to generate operational efficiencies

Not to belittle talent, but the wide expanse between IT and business results from the lack of common language and mission. The IT speak in the previous list illustrates that IT and the business are not in the same business—as most of us have experienced.

The business speaks of sales and expenses, whereas IT speaks of systems and technology. As such, it should be no surprise that the typical data scientist is limited in business acumen; thus, engaging the data scientist to implement AI in the business first requires educating them about the business.

For example, a Director of Inventory of a major technology company recounted an exercise in attempting to engage data scientists to develop an application that could yield insights from their data. The amount of time and effort it took to educate the data scientists about the business was so exhausting that the project was abandoned.

The myth of AI and analytics requiring data scientists emanates from the notion that business users lack requisite skills (formal training in mathematics, statistics, and specialized programming languages). This is certainly true for projects that use AI platforms where a combination of data scientists, database administrators, and application programmers is required. However, these complexities can be mitigated with modern AI-enabled analytics software tools that empower business users to engage analytics on their data without incurring the costs and complexities associated with platforms and tools that require specialized resources.

SHOT IN THE DARK

Another myth of analytics is the need to start with a "discovery" project, which retains a consultant to identify opportunities for the application of analytics. A recommended list of about a half-dozen pilot projects is prepared, each of which has a specified objective, budget, resources, and target return. However, it is to be determined whether the analytics can be developed and/or the return achieved, as this will have to wait until the pilot is well underway or completed before the values can be measured. We call this the *shot in the dark*, as the applicability and/or ROI of any recommended project is ambiguous at its start.

We consider that there is a low to medium risk of no ROI with this approach because there is so much low-hanging fruit for the application of analytics. However, this is an unnecessarily long, complex, and expensive journey, which ultimately increases the risk to achieving a successful implementation.

A side myth to note regards software vendor selection, in that consultants are not the objective arbiters of technology that they often claim to be. They have made significant investments to learn a few software products. This is not a bad practice; it is just that no one should be surprised when a consultant's recommendation of a software vendor happens to be one of their partners.

Note, too, that we are not advocating against consultants. Quite the contrary: consultants are an important part of the landscape for implementing an Analytics Culture. In fact, as we will discuss later, consultants are too often under-utilized for their expertise in business processes that the business critically needs to develop.

Analytics are best implemented by the business, and to avoid the shot in the dark, the business should identify its priorities—for after all, who knows more about the business's needs? From here, the business should select and work directly with the analytics software vendor. These folks know their product and its business applications. They can also bring consultants whom they consider best fitted to the customer. With this method, the business, not the consultant, is in charge—and that will bring focus, speed, cost efficiency, and lower risk to implementing analytics.

BASS-ACKWARD

A director for a technology venture accelerator asked two of his portfolio companies that had AI products to help him with a problem he thought AI could solve in his venture portfolio management. The director was in the middle of describing his problem when the founder of one company said the solution was using ML with JSON. The founder of the other AI company said, "Hold on! We don't even know the problem yet, to know what technology to bring to bear."

This is a common error for people in technology: putting technology in front of the problem. It is like bringing plumbing tools before knowing if the problem is plumbing or carpentry. This is simply a backward approach to problem solution, affectionately known as *bass-ackward*.

By focusing on technology first, the business problem or optimization being sought becomes secondary. The quest becomes finding people with skills who know the technology selected and tools that run the technology. Once found, they are given the "secondary" task to solve the problem; but their interest lies in using the technology, not in solving the problem. These people want to be clever about what the technology can do vs. curious about what insights can be gained from the data. This gap often manifests itself in more limited results for the business.

In combination with leaping to a particular technology is making the solution overly complex. For example, I sat with a PhD statistician at a large telecom company discussing demand forecasting. I had selected a particular forecast formula using a single variable to forecast demand from historical shipment data. Back-testing confirmed greater accuracy than was being achieved by the company's current method. The statistician wanted a similar forecast formula but with multiple variables and using as data inputs two other forecasts: the internal forecast and customer forecast.

His theory was that the internal forecast skewed lower than actual demand and the customer forecast skewed higher; thus, the blend should yield a more accurate forecast. I opined that this approach of using two forecasts to make a third forecast was like two drunks trying to help each other home. He disagreed, and I wished him well in his efforts to prove his methodology.

As predicted, the statistician's efforts were unfruitful, and when we resumed our talks, he now wanted to manipulate my formula by adding more variables. I reminded him that the forecasts achieved with my method had materially better accuracy and we were now pressed for time to deploy a forecast. The adage we should heed is, a good plan today is better than a perfect plan tomorrow.

Nevertheless, the statistician said he would not accept any forecast that was not multi-variable and that he could not manipulate, regardless of the accuracy of the results. He was focused on mathematics for the sake of mathematics and not the accuracy of the forecast for business. At this point, I wished him well and departed his company for the last time.

Einstein said, "Everything should be made as simple as possible, but not simpler."[4] Wise words that all statisticians and data scientists should heed, as leading with their ego to show everyone how smart they are only introduces complexity that ultimately breeds error. The solution to bass-ackward remains for the business and its users to define the problem and drive the analytics solution.

AI IS NOT IT

It is natural to think that anything with computers is the domain of IT. True, but only to a point. Think of IT as the Department of Transportation that makes the rules of the road, like weight and height limits of vehicles. The DOT does not, say, tell a trucking company what trucks it can or cannot buy. Similarly, IT should set policies for data security and software support but not decide what software a user can use.

IT should provide computing infrastructure and security for the data, but the choice of the software must be up to the user, as long as the software complies with the policies. However, IT usually becomes a roadblock by interjecting itself in the decision process. How many times have users found software that meets their needs wonderfully, only to be told by IT that they cannot have it because IT does not want to support it, or they must accept software already in-house, or they must use other software chosen by IT, or IT will build the software?

IT's job is to support the user who knows best what software will meet the business's needs. For example, a division of a Fortune 500 consumer package goods (CPG) company's demand planning group invited four software vendors to bid to provide demand forecasting. After proof-of-concept tests and bids from the vendors, the user group rejected one vendor and rated the other three for the gold, silver, and bronze medals. However, the vendor that won was selected by IT and was the vendor that was rejected by the users—twice!

The consequence of IT dominance in software selection is typically software that, in the best case, underperforms because it does not fully meet the business needs, and in the worst case is modestly used or goes unused. As such, when selecting analytics tools, be sure the choice is that of the users, not IT, or the value obtained will be marginal.

BIG IS NOT BETTER

There is a tendency, especially with IT, to "boil the ocean" on big data AI and analytics projects. While these can deliver a high return to the business, they are complex, long, and expensive, with price tags that only larger companies can afford. The risks are higher in this approach as it has many moving parts that require the integration of large infrastructure and people with specialized technical skills to communicate, coordinate, and collaborate with people who know the business to define the requirements and deliver a usable application.

However, analytics need not start here. In fact, it is better to start with a small to mid-size project because it is fast to value—and that value, when seen by others, begets the buy-in for more value, and so on. Smaller size also means lower cost, complexity, and risk.

A great start is simply automating existing spreadsheet reports in AI-enabled analytics tools. This has three immediate benefits: (i) it frees staff bandwidth by automating much of their time-consuming manual work in compiling spreadsheet reports; (ii) once the data is in the analytics tool, you get the analytics on the data as a by-product; and (iii) when staff reclaim bandwidth and have analytics, they now have time to explore their data to reveal insights for better decisions and planning.

This approach enables the rapid institutionalization of analytics: that is, since the reports to be automated are already part of the business process, the medium by which reporting is created becomes part of that process, too. So, without consciously launching analytics, you have launched analytics.

This is the most powerful technique for executives to employ to start analytics, and it is the path with the lowest cost, shortest time, and lowest risk as it involves the least amount of organizational change management.

NOT NOW

A particular affliction of many finance departments is to delay starting analytics because finance struggles with basic financial reporting and month-end close. The thinking is that if these rudimentary tasks cannot get done timely, accurately, and with accessibility to support operations, then the very function of finance is questionable. However, if the financial planning and analysis (FP&A) group of the finance organization is not ushering in AI and analytics to be a hub of predictive intelligence for planning, then it provides no modern value for business performance improvement.

As such, FP&A can and must leap-frog to analytics to both solve current reporting and advance to data-driven decisions, or it will be side-lined to routine tasks. In this configuration, the consequence is that finance is nothing more than a bean counter. The excuse that basic reporting comes before analytics or that difficulty with basic reporting precludes analytics is just that—an excuse. Finance can solve standard reporting and accommodate analytics using modern analytics and data visualization tools to both automate reporting and deliver analytics insights.

An analogy to this approach can be found in Third World countries in the 1990s and early 2000s that had poor telecom infrastructure. Instead of spending limited capital to upgrade and expand landlines, the jump was made to new cellular technology. It was faster and lower cost and shot them forward into the twenty-first century.

Using analytics tools to replace spreadsheet reports is a similar approach, as it accommodates the foundational business reporting; then, once the data is in the analytics tool, reports leap-frog to reveal added insights that can be found from the data. This approach is not limited to finance: all areas of the business that are awash in spreadsheets can use analytics tools in the same manner.

NOTE TO EXECUTIVES

The adage that software projects need executive support is very true in analytics, as analytics will change decisions, and change requires executive leadership. Executives, even when they want to develop a data-driven culture, often diminish or destroy its implementation.

The primary failure of analytics projects comes from executives who do not accept the use of analytics, perceive its benefits, have clarity of vision and understanding of AI/analytics, or have the leadership to discipline their companies to build an Analytics Culture.

Here is a true tale of a CEO (we will call him Jimmy) who runs a CPG manufacturing company (we will call it JimCo) of about $500 million that sells its products to distributors that then resell the products to retailers. In this business model, the shipments of products from JimCo to its distributors are known as *shipments*, and the shipments from the distributor to the distributor's retailers are called *depletions*. In this case, JimCo has data on both shipments and depletions.

Jimmy was forward-thinking to use ML to forecast depletions. The AI model worked well and had a last recorded accuracy for the full year 2020 of 93% across a representative swath of the company's business.

The company installed new master planning software for manufacturing that required increased accurate forecasts of shipments. While the ML forecast worked well for depletions, the characteristics of shipment data were significantly different, and the ML algorithm yielded materially lower accuracy of 86% across the same swath of business.

In search of better shipment forecast accuracy, the manager in charge of the depletion forecast (we will call him Bert) found a software company with a new approach to AI forecasting and ran a proof-of-concept (POC) test. Figure 3.1 displays the percent error of the forecast made 12 months in advance by the new POC software compared to the existing ML model across five major SKUs. As presented, the POC software achieved materially higher forecast accuracy for shipments across three of the SKUs and overall had a total error of only about 5% one year in advance (95% accuracy) vs. the ML model with a 14% error (86% accuracy).[5]

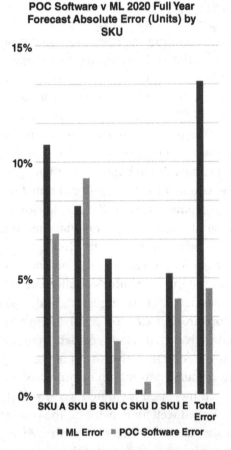

Figure 3.1 Forecast error comparison.

Further, the POC was extended to depletions, where the POC software achieved forecast accuracy to 99% vs. the ML model's 93%.

This POC software also had other extensive AI-enabled analytics applications that could add significant benefits in sales, finance, and inventory.

The new analytics software was brought to Jimmy's attention. However, Jimmy's response was, essentially, to counsel Bert to "stay in his lane," as requests for business improvements should be initiated from the business units.

It is understandable that Jimmy is hesitant to drive change, since change is the hardest item to tackle; but ignoring material benefits to business performance lacks prudence and is counter to the CEO role of continuously improving his business's performance.

So, in wonderful simplicity, it is down to the CEO (or business unit executive) to make analytics a part and priority of the business. A paper from McKinsey & Company, "A CEO guide for avoiding the ten traps that derail digital transformations," by Arun Arora et al., makes this point and tags the top three CEO mistakes: Excess Caution, Fear of Unknown, and Lack of Focus.[6]

In Chapter 6, we will discuss the three essential responsibilities for executives to achieve an Analytics Culture: *focus*, *budget*, and *bandwidth*. *Focus* is keeping the organization on the tactical Roadmap, which executives typically derail with special projects. *Budget* is simply allocating sufficient funds to buy AI-enabled software and train people; but too often, executives attempt to "cheap" a solution by restricting software or training. *Bandwidth* is enabling staff with the time to learn the tools and apply the techniques of analytics; yet executives will not relieve staff of any responsibility, and instead, staff must work harder to incorporate a new scope without any supporting resources.

Executives must make the jump from just seeing data and reporting information to decisions from unbiased predictions of the future. Those who react to the future when the future arrives face certain peril from those who use AI-enabled analytics to plan to make the future happen.

CONCLUSION

By being aware of myths and misconceptions about analytics, executives will be able to methodically, efficiently, and effectively implement a culture of data-driven decisions from AI and accelerate business performance.

With few exceptions, executives are leaving at least 5 to 10% better business performance on the table due to under-optimized planning. This is often a matter of choice when an executive has an attitude that good enough is good enough. But why settle for a dime of cost avoidance when spending a dollar on analytics can gain you 10?

Executives of the company, division, group, or department will determine the future of their business. It is up to you to lead the business into the future where AI-enabled analytics is certain to be required. The faster the adoption of AI, the more certain that you will secure a competitive position for yourself and your company.

NOTES

1. BrainyQuote. (n.d.) George Orwell quotes. https://www.brainyquote.com/quotes/george_orwell_377904.
2. Ritchie, E.J. (2016). Fact checking the claim of 97% consensus on anthropogenic climate change. *Forbes*. https://www.forbes.com/sites/uhenergy/2016/12/14/fact-checking-the-97-consensus-on-anthropogenic-climate-change/?sh=3490e7101157.
3. Peres, J. (2013). No clear link between passive smoking and lung cancer. *NCI: Journal of the National Cancer Institute* 105 (24): 1844–1846. https://doi.org/10.1093/jnci/djt365.
4. BrainyQuote. (n.d.). Albert Einstein quotes. https://www.brainyquote.com/quotes/albert_einstein_103652.
5. Aurora Predictions, LLC. (2021). AI forecasting & comparisons. Unpublished work.
6. Arora, A., Dahlstrom, P., Groover, P., and Wunderlich, F. (2017). A CEO guide for avoiding the ten traps that derail digital transformations. McKinsey. https://www.mckinsey.com/~/media/McKinsey/Business%20Functions/McKinsey%20Digital/Our%20Insights/A%20CEO%20guide%20for%20avoiding%20the%20ten%20traps%20that%20derail%20digital%20transformations/A-CEO-guide-for-avoiding-ten-traps.ashx.

CHAPTER 4

Applications of AI-Enabled Analytics

*There are very few personal problems that cannot be
solved through the suitable application of high explosives.*

—Scott Adams[1]

The McKinsey Global Institute estimates that "data and analytics could create value worth between $9.5 trillion and $15.4 trillion a year if embedded at scale."[2] So why has analytics adoption been so slow?

According to the annual global benchmark survey *Temperature of Finance*, from the Finance Analytics Institute, the 2021 survey paints a bleak picture of the current adoption of analytics, as presented in Figure 4.1.[3] Starting at the top of the chart is the *Persona* called the *Reporter*, defined as someone who reports data. The term *Persona* relates to the *Mindset* in the decision process. Reporters have the Mindset to *Support* decisions with data reporting. Next is the *Commentator*, with the Mindset to *Contribute* to decisions by reporting information. The *Advisor* follows, with the Mindset to *Influence* decisions with insights from low-level analytics; and the *Strategist* has the Mindset to *Impact* decisions with insights and foresight from AI-enabled advanced analytics.

The survey is a self-assessment using a series of questions to rate performance relating to capabilities in each of the Personas: Reporter, Commentator, Advisor, and Strategist. The three capabilities referenced in the chart are the Analytics Toolbox, referring to a range of tools beyond spreadsheets to AI-enabled analytics; Strategic Leadership, about formulating company strategy; and the Partnering Skillset, regarding communication and collaboration across the different areas of the business.

Each Persona has incrementally more analytics, leadership, and business partnering capabilities than the next Persona, going clockwise from the Reporter. However, the survey reveals marginally passing grades (C and D) for the Reporter and Commentator. The Advisor and Strategist rate a failing grade (F), especially for the Analytics Toolbox that applies AI and analytics on data beyond spreadsheets and data visualization tools. Most disturbing is the very wide gap between a passing grade (D) and the current failing grade of the Analytics Toolbox.

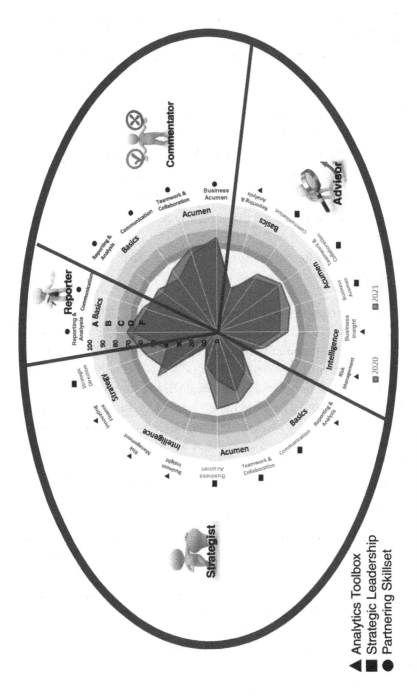

Figure 4.1 Benchmark analytics business partner.

The slow uptake of analytics in finance, which extends to most other business areas, can be distilled into seven "reasons" often given for delaying or avoiding analytics. These are presented next, along with our responses:

1. Now is not the right time. *If not now, then when?*
2. It's too expensive. *So are bad/uninformed decisions.*
3. I don't have the budget. *Really? Not $1 to make $10?*
4. We don't have the expertise. *Then hire those who do.*
5. We need an immediate ROI. *What does "immediate" mean?*
6. Our current tools are sufficient. *Really? Your business is running perfectly?*
7. Digital transformation sounds complex. *So is bankruptcy when you're competitively crushed.*

While our responses seem terse, they are accurate. There will never be a good time to start anything if all that is seen are obstacles vs. opportunities. My grandfather would say, "The hardest part of a project is starting it." How true! Whether it is a new product launch, an acquisition, or adding a new manufacturing line, anything new is never a good time to start and never a better time to take a step into the future.

ROI happens after analytics are integrated into the business decision process, so the sooner analytics is started to make data-driven decisions, the sooner ROI will result. And analytics is *not* expensive when compared to the alternative of uninformed decisions and under-optimized planning.

Think about your own decision-making experiences. Often, we refer to a single point in history to support our decision, like, "I remember when Bobby said we'd get the Johnson deal and it didn't happen, so let's shave 5% from next year's sales target." These are qualitative and biased (System 1 thinking) decisions and do not utilize unbiased analytics on data (for System 2 thinking).

As such, business too often reacts to the future when it arrives rather than planning to make the future happen. This leads to under-optimized planning that we conservatively estimate costs North American businesses some $240 billion annually![4]

And what about that toolbox? As in most departments, Excel is the primary tool for reporting, analysis, and planning. Departments that have data visualization largely use it to automate spreadsheet reports and for dashboards. Budgeting tools are good for consolidated reporting, but these are not analytics tools. Legacy business intelligence (BI) tools have essentially become data-marts for other reporting and data visualization tools.

If you combined all the users and uses of all the BI, budgeting, and data visualization tools on the planet, it would not come close to all the users and uses of Excel. But why, if these other tools are so much more powerful and valuable, do they not have broader adoption? Simple: Excel is so widely used because it can be! We all have it, and we all know how to use it.

All other tools have learning curves, often require IT support, and have relatively long implementation times. But we can all build a spreadsheet on the fly; and when asked for a report, our response is, "I can do that in a minute." Then we suffer through the follow-on labor of data collection, maintenance, rigidity, clumsiness, lack of standards, errors, security failures, data governance gaps, and so on. What is gained in ease and speed of creating the initial report is lost in spades everywhere else.

So, while budgeting and data visualization tools can add value to operations, they are primarily hindsight-looking and dramatically short of the AI-enabled analytics needed to gain the deep insights that can move the business's needle. While these tools should be part of the toolbox, they will not complete the toolbox. For that, modern AI-enabled analytics tools are required.

You cannot build a house with only a hammer, and the same is true to exploit data for insights. You will simply have to expand your tools and people skills. Business that fails to go beyond Excel or that limits the toolbox to a particular tool is doomed to fall short of insights.

Even for the same type of tool, there may need to be multiple products. Again, referring to the house analogy, there is not just one type of hammer. Similarly, there are different types of software tools that better fit the application of use and user. For example, doing research in drug interactions is vastly different than optimizing freight costs in both the application of use and the type of user. There is simply no one-size-fits-all tool, even within the same category of tool, and failing to understand this will reduce or inhibit the ROI from analytics.

We have highlighted the key issues that deter the implementation of analytics, and a remedy is to now discuss some of the many uses of analytics that can give incentive for its deployment. Note that the following examples in finance, sales, manufacturing, supply chain, and demand planning and inventory are by no means comprehensive or complete. We have selected areas where AI-enabled analytics can have great value and is typically underutilized. Areas like marketing are not included because they have been at the forefront of analytics (especially with web and ecommerce analytics). Robotic process automation (RPA) is also not discussed because it is process automation and not analytics for insights (although RPA is recommended, especially for routine functions like accounts payable [AP] and accounts receivable [AR] for cost savings and time efficiency).

FINANCE

An enlightening paper from McKinsey & Company in August 2020, "Predictive sales forecasting: Is your finance function up to code?" by Holger Hurtgen et al. discusses the application of analytics in finance:

> Most executives will tell you that when shaping
> business plans and strategy, forecasts can serve as a great
> counterweight to gut feelings and biases. Most will also
> admit, however, that their forecasts are still notoriously
> inaccurate. There are signs, however, that some finance
> teams' early experiments with automation, machine
> learning, and advanced analytics are changing the game—
> particularly for demand planning and sales-and-revenue
> forecasts. A chemical distributor, for instance, increased
> its sales by 6 percent because of its ability to conduct more
> accurate and frequent forecasts that informed its allocation
> of resources. A retailer and a global engineering-consulting
> firm both reported similar benefits from advanced
> analytics, as measured by user responses to new products
> and by changes in profit on income, respectively.

Finance is typically a technology laggard as it stubbornly resists expanding beyond spreadsheets. Finance has a hand in a multitude of areas that can drive business performance, including:

- Budgeting
- Rolling forecasts
- Long-range planning
- Sales and operating planning (S&OP)
- Revenue quality assurance
- Cost optimization

AI-enabled analytics can have a central role in finance, to go beyond the "trusted scorekeeper" and to a strategic partner, as it can enable finance to move past its traditional focus of cost control and into top-line growth. This is important because finance naturally has good communication throughout the business and is the go-to department for financial data.

Budgeting is a stellar use for analytics as the typical budget is DOA. This is not to discount the budgeting process as a valuable exercise, but to state what we all know: budgets do not survive first contact with reality. The key issue is the top line, as this is the area business cannot meticulously control as it can costs.

Demand, sales, and revenue are all subject to the customer. But the good news is that customer prediction is in the realm of analytics, often with accuracy superior to biased human guesses that are made in the budgeting process.

But you say, "My budgeting tool forecasts revenue." There is a significant difference between allocating a guess, which is typically done with budgeting tools vs. statistical forecasting that can mitigate bias, and the truly unbiased forecasting from AI enablement. And for the latter, you'll need AI-enabled tools.

This is not to say AI tools replace budgeting tools; rather, they work in concert with the workflow capabilities of budgeting tools and the input of future events that humans know but that are not contained in the data. This is the best of all worlds that combine man-and-machine.

Further, advanced analytics can greatly impact how to plan and react to the future. In Figure 4.2, a Monte Carlo simulation forecasts the future *range* of possible outcomes for the units sold to distributors for Product SKU A. Rather than a point forecast that is almost always wrong, Monte Carlo provides statistical bands of probable outcomes that show the "risk" in the forecast: that is, instead of a human guessing that a forecast is accurate to plus/minus 10%, Monte Carlo calculates the statistical probability of the range. The dark middle line represents the forecast, and each band is a *confidence interval* about the forecast. Having an unbiased calculation of forecast risk has wide application in long-range planning, inventory optimization, manufacturing planning, and service-level agreements.

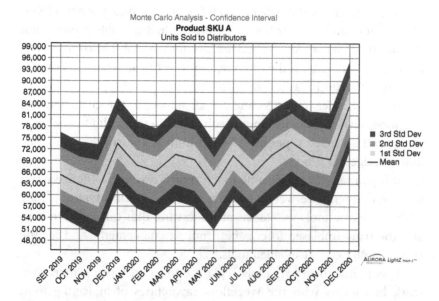

Figure 4.2 Monte Carlo simulation.

Another beautiful use of advanced analytics based on a Monte Carlo simulation is what we call the *Fair Challenge*. After all is said and done with the budget, or from time to time during the year, the CEO or other senior executive challenges for more top-line growth. The organization moans, and some departments weep with exasperation because what is being asked is not reasonable. Undeterred, the valiant executive pushes their troops for more top-line growth. The only remaining decision is whether the challenge will be allocated equally or proportionally.

While this is a common event, it is disruptive, with some folks perceiving that they are being targeted. It all seems unfair, and the CEO becomes a villain! Enter the Fair Challenge to rescue our hero executive.

The Fair Challenge, shown in Figure 4.3, applies advanced analytics to calculate the probability of attaining the new gross distributor sales forecast target across the company's distributors. The probability of making the challenge is based on a statistical analysis of the organization's past performance. An increase from the forecast current value of some $7.5 billion to a challenge value of $7.7 billion has an objective quantitative assessment of 20% probability of attainment, as marked by the horizontal solid line. Note that analytics of the challenge would be the same regardless of company size or industry, as it is statistically based on past performance.

It is now back to the executive to determine if they really want to tax their organization with a one-in-five shot at achievement. If the answer is yes, then the amount, in this example, is allocated among the distributors at the intersection of each distributor's curve and the solid line, so that each distributor has the same 20% probability of achievement—that is, a Fair Challenge. So, while MicroCenter has twice the total quota of Viking, MicroCenter's allocation is some $27 million of the $200 million challenge value increase, whereas Viking's is $17 million. In this way, all understand their odds, and all have the same odds, so no one feels targeted; and all have the same probability of succeeding, even with non-proportional allocations.

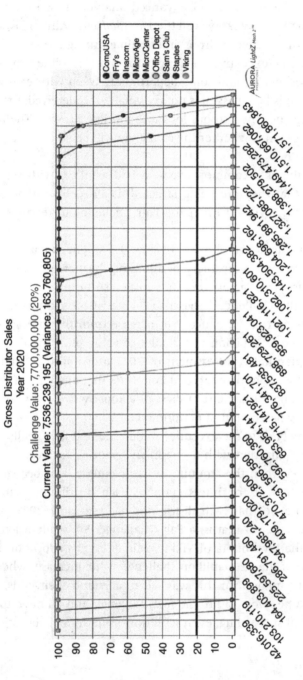

Figure 4.3 Fair Challenge.

SALES

There are many sales systems and tools, including CRM, revenue quality management, sales forecasting, and more. Some employ AI; however, CRM systems are the primary source to record all contacts between the sales rep and prospect, which makes the CRM rich with data for the applications of analytics.

For sales, finance, and manufacturing, knowing if and when a deal will close is paramount to revenue quality management, cash flow, and product delivery to the customer. All company activities flow downstream from the sale, and this is where AI-enabled analytics is highly valuable to predict whether a deal has a propensity to close when the sales rep forecasts it will.

Analytics can cull mountains of data by company, division, territory, product, sales rep, etc. to find characteristic patterns and thresholds to determine those that reveal when a deal is within a range to close. The analytics can group deals with a high, medium, or low propensity to close, to enable sales to best manage its resources.

Remember, the sales rep's "forecast" in the CRM software is the sales rep's guess; and while most organizations have disciplined sales assessment processes, a guess is still a guess. Advanced analytics can help triangulate to better decisions and identify the key data and factors that lead to a deal closing. For example, Figure 4.4 depicts the analytics path followed for each deal in a current sales pipeline. Sales forecasts from the CRM are entered into analytics software, which then performs calculations at each node to assess customer propensity to buy.[5]

The first two nodes assess (in comparison to a quantitative threshold) whether the prospect has a general "velocity" toward buying. The next node is a prediction of buying the current deal. The final node is a quantitative assessment of the relationship of five variables that rate the duration of the deal, size of the deal, stage of the deal, cadence of the deal, and flow of the deal. Accordingly, each deal can be placed in a bucket of high, medium, or low propensity to close in the current quarter.

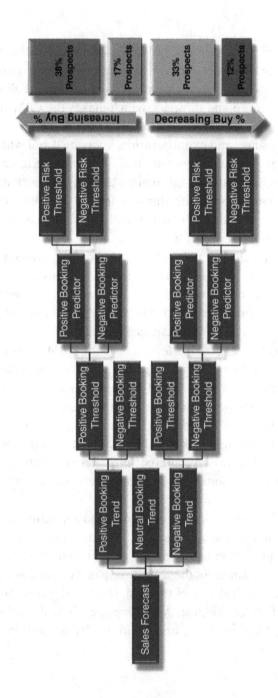

Figure 4.4 Sales deal path to close assessment.

Analytics assessments are objective, and while they are correct most of the time, they are not correct all of the time. For example, suppose Sales Rep Billy has a $1 million prospect in his pipeline projected to close in the next 45 days. He has dutifully taken his prospect through the sales steps and recorded those in the CRM. However, an analytical assessment of the CRM data calculates that the deal has a low propensity to close in the quarter as Billy has projected.

Undeterred, Billy says the deal will close, and when the clock is rolled forward, it does. However, this deal, and others like it, are usually accomplished with large discounts and/or concessions in order to meet self-imposed revenue recognition deadlines about the end of the quarter and year. These are the "unnatural" acts the company must live with that reduced cash flow and profit. It would have been financially better to extend the close date and allow the deal to complete "naturally" and have more profitable terms for the company.

In another common example, good sales reps are wrongly assigned to good customers. In the case of a large $1 billion division of a multinational technology company, analytics identified Sales Rep Bubba with an existing customer we will call Six Pack. Bubba has a tried-and-true record of selling deals in the $100,000 to $500,000 range, but the deal with Six Pack is for $5 million.

Along with a variety of characteristics, advanced analytics assessed that the deal would not close with Bubba, but sales management ignored the analytics. When the deal did not close as forecast by Bubba, a new sales rep was assigned who met the characteristics for the type of transaction, and the deal closed 30 days later.

MANUFACTURING AND SUPPLY CHAIN

As mentioned in the McKinsey paper, AI and analytics can have a material impact on demand planning, which is the trigger for the entire supply chain, from managing suppliers of materials to manufacturing to inventory to distribution to the ultimate customer and all connections in between. However, manufacturers experience an average demand forecast error of about 35%, which cascades to having an average excess and obsolete inventory of some 25%.[6,7] Add to this non-optimized inventory for both raw materials and finished product, and we estimate that North American businesses are leaving $182 billion annually on the table from under-optimized planning.[4] This despite over $500 billion spent annually by IT for enterprise software including ERP, CRM, POS, demand planning, supply chain, inventory, and so on, all of which is designed to resolve the very inefficiencies that continue to occur.[8]

A vice president in charge of a $1 billion supply chain for a Fortune 500 pharma company said, "I know my supply chain is broken, but I don't know where." He related that this problem is industry-wide, as although there has been an immense improvement from ERP software, people still do the last mile in spreadsheets. Essentially, all supply-chain planning ends up in someone's spreadsheet, and they make the final adjustments.

Smack in the middle of the supply chain is manufacturing, which is focused on optimization. The plant wants to run its lines with the highest efficiency to minimize costs that maximize profit. But plant optimization, product demand, and marketing promotions can be (and often are) in contention.

As such, the opportunity for the application of AI-enabled analytics in the supply chain and manufacturing is immense. For example, manufacturers that use bulk commodities in their finished products need to forecast the price of the commodity for standard product costing. If the forecast standard price is over-budgeted vs. the actual price, capital is trapped in manufacturing that could have been deployed in marketing. Utilizing AI forecasting for commodity prices often yields higher accuracy than internal guesses and many industry averages.

In the supply chain, the use of correlative analytics can expose disconnects: that is, where the flow of raw materials or finished products is not in sync between seller and buyer. For example, a correlation between finished products shipped from the manufacturer to the retailer that is not correlated with sales from the retailer to the consumer can indicate the supply chain is not in sync. The manufacturer is selling the finished product to the retailer at a different rate than the retailer is selling the product to consumers. This ultimately can result in the retailer having too much stock in inventory or being out of stock and missing sales (and lost sales from stock-outs are about 4% of a retailer's sales).[9]

DEMAND PLANNING AND INVENTORY

All business, whether making a product or selling a service, begins with the demand forecast. If the service is consulting, then a forecast of billable hours must be made against the resource capacity to deliver billable hours. If current capacity exceeds forecast billable hours for an extended period, a headcount reduction is often considered. And herein lies the problem with human biased forecasting. No one wants to be in the position to lay off people, so we gravitate to a higher forecast and ensure that our spreadsheets have a glowing picture of the future. It is better to let the future be the bad guy than anticipate the future and be blamed for over- or under-forecasting it.

In a multi-billion-dollar telecom company, chip demand was forecast on spreadsheets. In a clandestine manner, one person magically produced the 12-month and quarterly demand forecasts. As long as growth continued, all was good. Then, one quarter, demand dramatically slowed. The company was caught off guard, and heads rolled—except for the person who made the forecast. He was unscathed because he simply blamed the data used to make the forecast. Easy! Data accuracy was not his responsibility.

Even in "good times" of sustained growth, a price is paid in higher excess and obsolete (E&O) inventory, as the company's priority is to be sure it can always meet demand. Conversely, heaven help the demand planner who adjusts the forecast lower (to curb the allocation of capital tied up in inventory) after a sales rep calls the CEO to complain that he cannot make a sale for lack of inventory.

As such, optimized demand planning is about achieving a "Goldilocks" forecast: not too high, and not too low, but just right. And here, the application of advanced analytics yields high value. Enterprise demand planning software can increase demand forecast accuracy 20–30% over spreadsheets, but modern AI and analytics software incrementally adds another 20–40% accuracy over demand planning software.

Further, using Monte Carlo simulation produces an unbiased calculation of a range of forecast outcomes based on the statistical variability in the business. Monte Carlo's range of values is expressed as the statistical probability of the future outcome of those values.

Referring back to Figure 4.2, the first confidence interval of the middle band represents about a 68% probability that the future will fall within this interval. This can be used for manufacturing planning. Using the full width of the second and third confidence intervals outer bands has a probability of 95% and 99% that the future will fall within those bands, respectively. These wider bands offer best- and worst-case scenarios and can be deployed for inventory optimization.

For example, suppose the SKU in Figure 4.2 was so important that the business wanted to meet all future demand. In this case, the maximum stock level should be at the top of the third confidence interval, representing a 99% probability of meeting actual demand. In December, that amount would be about 95,000 units, but in May, that number is some 73,000 units. Using Monte Carlo, inventory levels can be set dynamically, thus saving large amounts of capital from being tied up in inventory.

In another example, a customer has negotiated a 95% service-level agreement. Using the same SKU, the inventory level is set at the top of the second confidence interval, which is dynamically adjusted from month to month to meet the SLA while minimizing inventory cost.

CONCLUSION

A business without AI-enabled analytics may be the best it can be, but if so, it is blind luck. When all you have are biased decisions, you have to rely on a modicum of luck that the decision has optimized business performance. Further, even with hundreds of billions of dollars spent in enterprise software every year, under-optimized planning resulting in financial underperformance remains the bill of fare. This is because these enterprise systems are transactional and not primarily analytical. Our research and experience reveals that AI-enabled analytics predictions and forecasts, with their unbiased and scientific calculations, can on average reduce broken supply chains, stock-outs, E&O inventory, and demand planning forecast error by 50%.[4]

NOTES

1. Art Quotes. (n.d.). Quotes about problems. www.art-quotes.com/getquotes.php?catid=243#.YLUW14WSlhE.

2. Ghia, A. and Langsta, M. (2021). Accelerating data and analytics transformations in the public sector. McKinsey & Company, Public & Social Sector.

3. Sorensen, J.H. and Zwerling, R.J. (2021). Temperature of finance 2021, assessing the finance journey to become an Analytics Business Partner. Finance Analytics Institute. www.fainstitute.com.

4. Aurora Predictions, LLC. (2020). Impact of under-optimized planning. Unpublished work.

5. Sorensen, J.H. and Zwerling, R.J. (2020). How to start an analytics project. Finance Analytics Institute, Analytics Academy.

6. E2Open. (2018). 2018 forecasting and inventory benchmark study. https://www.e2open.com/wp-content/uploads/2019/02/2018_Forecasting_and_Inventory_Benchmark_Study_white_paper_digital.pdf.

7. Smith, T. (n.d.). How to reduce excess and obsolete inventory. Numerical Insights, LLC. https://www.numericalinsights.com/blog/how-to-reduce-excess-and-obsolete-inventory.

8. Liu, S. (2021). Enterprise software total worldwide expenditure 2009-2022. Statista. https://www.statista.com/statistics/203428/total-enterprise-software-revenue-forecast.

9. Corsten, D. and Gruen, T. (2004). Stock-outs cause walkouts. *Harvard Business Review*. https://hbr.org/2004/05/stock-outs-cause-walkouts.

PART
II

Roadmap

CHAPTER **5**

Roadmap for How to Implement AI-Enabled Analytics in Business

Success is not final, failure is not fatal: it is the courage to continue that counts.

—Winston Churchill[1]

With the fundamentals of analytics in place and an enlightening discussion on human decision-making to espouse why analytics are essential, we now come to the core: the Roadmap to implement AI-enabled analytics. This chapter will deliver, in great detail, the "how to" for implementing a culture of data-driven decisions for improved business performance.

Geoffrey Moore, the famed organizational theorist and author of the book *Crossing the Chasm*, wrote, "Without big data analytics, you are blind and deaf and in the middle of a freeway."[2] As we shall now expound, it takes more than big data analytics to obtain the value of insights from data; it takes a *culture* about analytics; that is, it is one thing to reveal insights, and another to actively use them.

Insights are distinguished from *data* and *information*. As presented in Figure 5.1, data is simply the raw values collected from data sources. Information results from arithmetic manipulation, however small, that tells us more than the raw values. For example, subtracting the values of last year's sales year-to-date against this year's sales informs whether year-over-year sales have increased or decreased. This is information from data. But when AI-enabled analytics is applied on data, insights are obtained that reveal something that we do not know about our business and that, when known, will influence decisions.

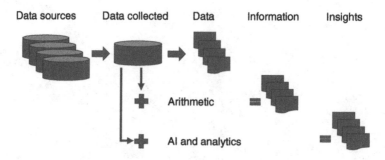

Figure 5.1 From data to insights.

While the preponderance of articles and books talk about what AI and analytics are, they often fail to inform the reader how to engage AI and build a culture that can find and make use of the insights from the application of analytics on data. Sure, there is a mountain of case studies, but only a slice of readers will be able to know how to apply those to their business. Therefore, it is the mission of this book and this chapter to discuss the Roadmap of how to implement a *culture* of analytics.

Often, people associate analytics with the act of implementing an analytics tool. However, as defined in the Merriam-Webster Dictionary (https://www.merriam-webster.com/dictionary/culture), a culture is "the set of shared attitudes, values, goals, and practices that characterizes an institution or organization." As such, we must go beyond merely selecting a tool and recognize the imperative to incorporate people and practices as well. Therefore, we define the *Analytics Culture* as

---

Mindset, People, Processes, and Systems to make data-driven decisions from quantitative analytics and predictions

---

The four items listed in the definition are the components of the culture used in decision-making; such decisions incorporate analytics and predictions. Let us now learn about the culture and its components so we may formulate a Roadmap.

CULTURE

Returning to the McKinsey paper referred to in Chapter 3, "A CEO Guide for Avoiding the Ten Traps that Derail Digital Transformations," number 5 is lack of talent:

> Most companies embarking on digital transformations underestimate how long it takes to build capabilities. They know they need digital talent, but not what kind or how much. A digital transformation at a large company can require as many as 150 full-time employees in the first year. Hiring a chief digital [officer] is a good start but is not enough.

Any effective talent search should begin with identifying the problems that need to be solved. This helps clarify the skill sets you need. After a preliminary analysis, for example, one company determined that it needed 11 people with specific skill sets—"leaders" and "doers"—to complete a core project as part of a transformation. It found the right people at a leading tech company and paid a 100 percent premium to hire them. Later in the transformation, the next 50 people came at just a 20 percent premium because they were eager to work with the first hires. In less than nine months, the team generated $1.4 billion in incremental annualized revenues, a massive payoff for what had originally seemed a disproportionate investment.

Great Scott! Hiring 150 people and paying a 100% premium on the first 11 for one "core" project is out of the ballpark for the vast majority of companies, especially when considering that only about 20,000 businesses out of some 6 million in the US have more than 500 employees.[3] Further, how many companies could—and which executive would take the risk to—go down this very expensive path without knowing if it would bear fruit, only to find it could not be done or the benefits were less than the staggering costs?

However, suppose we could afford this project and were willing to undertake the risk. What defines the right people, where to find them, and which skills make one person a leader and another a doer? When the people are hired, what will they do with the tools bought for them? Are the people expected to know your business and what is needed for business optimization? If they give you what you want, will you know how to use it?

These are some of the unanswered questions when analytics is approached as a specific project to retain certain talent for a specific outcome. This is not a culture. The culture of the application of AI-enabled analytics on data is more than just, well, the application of AI-enabled analytics on data. It includes how you absorb analytics in business, the evolution of data in analytics to gain better and deeper insights, and having the processes to incorporate insights into decisions. It is more than just tools and talent; it is building a culture about the four blocks: *Mindset, People, Process,* and *Systems.*

MINDSET

Mindset is an attitude toward the decision-making process and includes *Support, Contribute, Influence,* and *Impact.* To *Support* decisions means to *Report* the data. To *Contribute* to decisions, *Analysis* (the application of arithmetic on data) is integral to the reporting. To *Influence* decisions requires at least high-level *Insight.* To *Impact* decisions requires deep analytics to gain *Insight* or *Predict.*

Report, Analysis, Insight, and *Predict* are the four levels of *Analytics Intelligence.* Each level increases in value to decision-making from what was to what will be. The adage "If I knew then what I know now, I would have made a different decision" is the path of Analytics Intelligence.

In Figure 5.2, Analytics Intelligence intersects with the five key questions for decision-making: "What happened? "Where did it happen?" "Why did it happen?" "What will happen?" and "How to make it happen?" Each question is related to a Mindset and associated with a *Persona.*[4]

The first question asks the *Reporter* Persona to report data: e.g. sales were $1 million. The second question involves a level of analysis as a *Commentator*: e.g. sales were down 5% due to three stores in Los Angeles. An *Advisor* can deliver analytics to yield insights: e.g. sales are down 5% because unemployment in Los Angeles is up and unemployment is negatively correlated with sales. The final two questions are about the future and are the realm of the *Strategist* Persona. They can be answered with AI-enabled analytics: e.g. sales are statistically forecast to continue to be down for the next six months, but correlations with price show that a 10% discount will increase sales even with current or 0.5% higher unemployment.

As depicted in Figure 5.3, the first two questions are *Informative;* but decisions are made from applying analytics to answer the last three questions, which are *Insightful.* As such, Reporter and Commentator Personas connect to the Informative quadrants, which *Support* and *Contribute* to decisions. However, the Advisor and Strategist Personas are associated with the Insightful quadrant, which includes the drivers to *Influence* and *Impact* decisions.

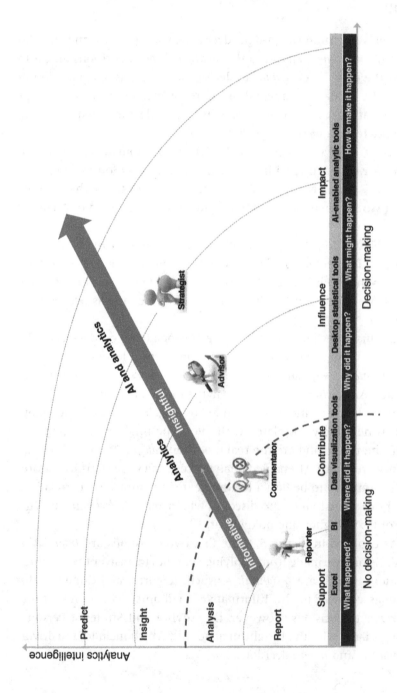

Figure 5.2 Analytics Intelligence, decisions, and Personas

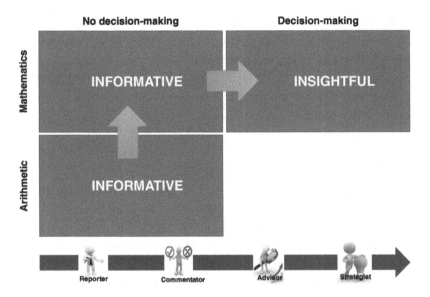

Figure 5.3 Informative vs. Insightful

Each Persona is associated with its Mindset toward decision-making. Thus, Mindset must be aligned across the organization, or the Analytics Culture cannot be created. For example, a Senior Director of Finance of a major pharma company saw a demo of AI-enabled analytics software. The director perceived great value in using the tool to automate many functions done in Excel, like long-range planning. Once the data was in the tool, he would get analytics insights from the data for "free"—it was two mints in one.

The director wanted to do a proof-of-concept (POC) test with the analytics vendor, but before the test started, the director left for another company. The replacement director asked the vendor to demo the software to low-level Excel jockeys. However, given the staff's Mindset, they saw no value in automating something they could already do in spreadsheets, and insights from analytics were irrelevant as they were not decision-makers. As such, following the demo, everyone wished each other well, and the financial planning and analysis (FP&A) department remained with spreadsheets.

The issues here are two-fold. First, we do not know if the replacement director had a Mindset for analytics, but by assigning the evaluation to low-level staff, we do know the director had no leadership to engage an Analytics Culture. Second, the staff of Excel jockeys were comfortable as Reporters and had no Mindset to adopt analytics, regardless of whether the director had such a Mindset. So, in both cases, there was a failure of Mindset alignment and leadership to pursue the Analytics Culture.

PEOPLE

People are needed to run analytics tools and prepare reports. Right? Right—but there is more. To build a culture requires more than a person and a machine. A culture requires *people*, the plural of *person*. If an Analytics Culture consists of one tool and one person, we affectionately refer to this as *Bobby in the basement*.

Suppose Mr. Big, the CEO, calls Bobby to say, "Bobby, Sally in sales is telling me we'll close the year with $1 million in new sales. What does your analytics tool tell you?" Bobby does his work and then calls Mr. Big to say, "Yep, $1 million looks good."

After that interchange, what does Mr. Big do? When all you have is Bobby, there is nothing more to do than feel good about Sally's guess. However, a culture requires people using analytics in the decision process to *mobilize company resources for better planning and performance outcomes*. Bobby in the basement is void of the organization of people in a process that methodically uses AI-enabled analytics for planning and business performance improvement.

People need to have what we call *hard* and *soft* skills to properly implement AI and analytics that achieve the Analytics Culture. *Hard* refers to capabilities related to using AI and analytics software that yields insights and goes beyond the Excel jockey. *Soft* refers to capabilities related to thinking, communicating, and collaborating.

From our research and experience, we have developed the pie chart in Figure 5.4, showing these soft skills: *Curious, Analytical, Consultive, Collaborative,* and *Communicative. Curious* means to wonder what insights data may reveal, and *Analytical* refers to a systematic thought process to approach and solve a problem or optimize a process. *Consultative* is the approach to inform, train, and interactively listen when interfacing within your department and with other departments. This feeds into the ability to be *Collaborative* to knowledgeably interface across the business in decision-making. And *Communicative* is the storytelling capability that engages managers so they may absorb the insights from analytics used to make their decisions.

People soft skills

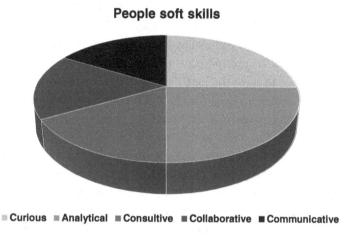

▨ Curious ▪ Analytical ▪ Consultive ▪ Collaborative ▪ Communicative

Figure 5.4 People proportional soft skills.

When considering a company, division, group, or department, we assess the approximate proportion of time in each soft skill to support an Analytics Culture. We recommend that the first two attributes, Curious and Analytical, should compose some 50% of the organization's soft skills, as these summon analytical thinking within a mind that has a propensity for analytical thought. The other elements compose the other half of people's soft skills and represent the ability to interface within and between business areas to deliver and utilize insights from analytics.

If all you have are Excel jockeys, analytics will fail. The reason has as much to do with the incorrect tool for analytics as the difference in approach to data: an Excel jockey tends to be *clever* about Excel, whereas a business analyst tends to be *curious* about insights that can be gained from the data. This is a difference with a significant distinction.

When you ask your staff for a report, listen to their answers, as they will measure whether people are clever or curious. A clever staff will answer, "I can get that done in a minute." But a curious staff will respond, "What decision are you trying to make?" The former is thinking about how to get the tool to deliver the data, while the latter understands the insights needed to make a better-informed decision.

At an Analytics Academy of the Finance Analytics Institute, Keith Davidson, a former VP Finance at a major CPG company, related his experience when, upon the installation of a new ERP system, the CFO wanted to revamp the group to be more analytical. To that end, the group was restructured to have the best Excel jockeys. This proved to be a disaster, as Excel jockeys are clever about Excel and not curious about the insight the data contains, and thus the CFO failed to gain the value from analytics insights. The moral of this story is that you can teach people the skill of using a tool, but insights come from the mind of a curious person.

Also, you do not need to focus on hiring data scientists exclusively, as intelligent people can be taught any tool. Further, data scientists usually do not know the business, and significant effort needs to be expended to give them understanding of the optimization being sought. This often leads to the added cost of hiring consultants to define the problem for the data scientists.

Another inefficiency in building sufficient people for the Analytics Culture is the notion that new resources need to be hired. This thinking is based on the perception that to do analytics takes a special and dedicated person (because everyone is already working at capacity and has no bandwidth available for the added task of analytics). While it may be necessary to hire new or added talent, lack of bandwidth is caused by wasted labor collecting and cleaning data and compiling volumes of reports that are unused or little used and of little value. Eliminating wasteful reporting and then automating much of the rest can free an average of 50% of people's bandwidth.[5]

PROCESS

Process is intrinsically understood but institutionally weak. While business operates on processes, many of the things we do each day are based more on tradition than written procedures. To maximize the benefits of analytics for data-driven decisions, discipline from structured processes is required.

Processes are written procedures that take what is done by custom and memorialize it to enable any person in the organization to follow the role described in the procedure. This is how customs—routine tasks—become institutionalized.

Processes for analytics are in two main groups: *Data Governance* and *Decision Governance*.[4] The former is about ensuring that data used in decisions is accurate, complete, timely, and accessible. The latter regards the decision-making process itself and identifies the decision-making participants, steps, and authorities.

Processes are the easiest area to overlook and are typically shortchanged: these are seen as the last mile, and it is assumed that staff will complete this task. Guess what? Their plates are already full, and many parts of the last mile remain unfinished. This is a bridge to nowhere that is completely avoidable. Use external implementation resources, like consultants, and get the whole job done.

Written procedures are the stuff that creates institutionalization. While it seems bureaucratic, it is essential for sustaining the culture; otherwise, when Bobby in the basement leaves the company, analytics will leave along with him. Process ensures that more people are involved and supports the continuity of Data and Decision Governance when people leave.

Data Governance

Data accuracy is the responsibility of everyone and not, as many people perceive, the sole purview of IT. Does IT know if GL data is wrong? Does IT know if the demand plan forecast is reasonable? Does IT know if BigCo is not an active customer? Of course not! Then why would IT have the primary responsibility for data governance, if it cannot assess the most important part of data governance—data accuracy? The primary responsibility for data governance flows from the users of the data, and it is not one person's job but *part* of the job of *every* individual.

For data to be accurate, complete, timely, and accessible, we need to know what data is needed, when it is needed, in what form it is needed, who consumes it, who controls it, and when and how it can be revised. All this is easily identified and memorialized in a written process to ensure that these essentials of Data Governance are adhered to in the normal course of operations.

Decision Governance

Next is Decision Governance, to make data-driven decisions. But, you say, we know how to make decisions, and we make them every day. Yes, but too often we do so by "gut." For example, how many meetings have we attended where spreadsheets and PowerPoints are passed around the room during the decision process? Conversations about the past abound as the team tries to divine a decision. Stories are told that often follow the same theme: "I remember last year when Billy said we would get $1 million in new sales, but we only got $500,000." In the end, small decisions tend to be made using spreadsheets of past high-level data, whereas large decisions are often made based on emotion. This is illustrative of the System 1 and System 2 thinking and behavioral groupthink discussed in Chapter 2.

In a culture of data-driven decisions by analytics, we impose a discipline on decisions that use mathematics on the past and unbiased predictive insights for the future. When decisions have a material impact on business performance, we must be informed with correlations to past events, analysis of current efficiencies, and objective insights into the future.

Decision Governance ensures that our intuition and experience align with dispassionate unbiased analytics to achieve the best possible decisions.

SYSTEMS

Systems are the tools used for reporting, analysis, and analytics and fall in two broad classifications: *Informative* and *Insightful*. Informative systems are associated with the Analytics Intelligence areas of Report and

Analysis, whereas Insightful systems achieve the Analytics Intelligence areas of Insight and Predict. Informative tools include spreadsheets, data visualization, and business intelligence (BI), while Insightful tools include desktop statistical software, cloud analytics platforms, and modern AI-enabled analytics software.

Excel is the uber-Informative tool because it is known by and available to essentially everyone. All other tools have a learning curve, often require specialized skills, and have a months-long implementation cycle, although Insightful tools provide the highest value for decision-making and business performance improvement.

We will now compare and contrast the tools of spreadsheets, data visualization, and AI-enabled analytics to facilitate a better understanding of the toolbox that needs to be developed to achieve an Analytics Culture. We will then discuss the development of the toolbox as associated with each Persona.

Spreadsheets

Spreadsheets are the fastest medium to build a new report, the most inefficient medium to maintain a report, and the most ineffective tool for AI-enabled analytics. However, because everyone knows Excel, it is terribly overused, to the exclusion of other tools that are far better suited for the business to gain insights. According to an IDC study, a staggering $60 billion is wasted annually in the labor associated with spreadsheets.[6]

From a practical perspective, large enterprise-scale models and applications built on spreadsheets are fraught with difficulty, as these are riddled with errors, lack best practices, have no Data Governance, and so on. In fact, a comprehensive 2009 study by STRATEGY@Risk cites that audits show "that nearly 90% of the spreadsheets contained *serious errors (emphasis added)*. Code inspection experiments also show that even experienced users have a hard time finding errors, succeeding in only finding 54% on average."[7] This is one of many studies that conclude what we all have experienced—that spreadsheets are stuffed with errors.

The Roadmap to an Analytics Culture demands a toolbox that brings the right tool to the right person for the right job. This is not to say we should do away with Excel. Quite the contrary; Excel is the most versatile tool in the toolbox. The problem is its overuse for seemingly everything and the endless work to build, enhance, operate, and maintain spreadsheets. This level of effort, which we refer to as Excel *suffocation*, prevents organizations from advancing to analytics.

For example, the Data Analytics group in a $1 billion technology company hires people in Eastern Europe to pull data from the BI data-mart after hours because the data pull is so large it takes nearly the entire day to process. This massive data set is then loaded into spreadsheets that are laboriously manipulated to prepare management reports—without insights! The shame is the man at the head of the group who has high-IQ talent doing low-IQ data and report compilation. He is a spreadsheet grunt with no time to use his curiosity to explore the data to discover insights that can better performance.

In the twenty-first century, being smothered by spreadsheets and largely manual tasks wastes valuable talent. The excuse often heard is that the data must be cleaned before it gets into the report, and somehow, someone must do this task each month because it cannot be automated. Poppycock. If data is incorrect, fix it at the source.

Data Visualization

Many executives are infatuated with dashboards and visualizations that are adorned with colors and charts but do not add any value to their decision-making. Instead, executives must get smart about tools—not become software experts, but know what tools are needed to produce insight for data-driven decisions.

As we have said, the arithmetical analysis provides information but not insight. Dashboards largely consist of displayed data. The associated arithmetic on the data is typically used as a health check of the current business state against its key performance indicators

(KPIs). This is informative but not Insightful as it does not affect decisions. To derive insights from data, mathematics is applied, but such application is not automatically Insightful unless it can be used to affect decisions.

Depicted in Figure 5.5 is an Executive Dashboard from a major data visualization tool vendor. While it is pretty, what decision is the dashboard supporting? Hard to say, as it is largely data with some arithmetic and looks more like a health check. It does not answer why a trend is in a particular direction or what the future of the trend is predicted to be. We see that 730 YTD incidents is more than last year, but the dashboard has no indication why incidents have increased or if this trend is predicted to increase or decrease. So, while we have pretty data and information, we do not have insights for decisions.

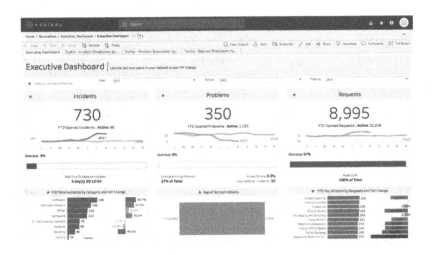

Figure 5.5 Tableau Executive Dashboard (https://www.tableau.com/solutions/it-analytics).

Data visualization vendors often claim their tools are analytics and suitable for data-driven decisions, but as we have said, analytics is created from the application of mathematics on data. However, what if a visualization tool applies mathematics as depicted in Figure 5.6?

Statistical trend lines show the relationship between sales and profits for three categories (Furniture, Office Supplies, and Technology). Is this now analytics?

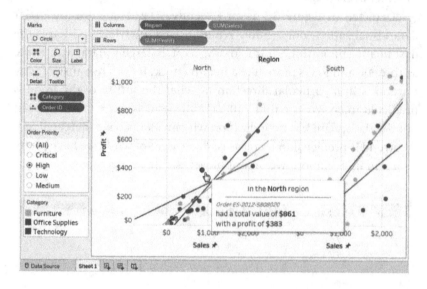

Figure 5.6 Tableau Dashboard (https://www.tableau.com/products/desktop).

No, because trend lines are *Informative*, not Insightful to affect decisions. No decisions can be made just from being Informative, as it only reveals *what happened*: for example, some orders are above the trend line (are generating more profit), while other orders are below the trend line. It also is informative about *where it happened*, noting that order ES-2012-5808020 in the Technology category has a data point in the North region above the Technology trend line.

But the dashboard does not determine *why it happened*, meaning why some Technology data points are above the Technology trend line and others are below it. The dashboard also does not predict *what will happen* or *how to make it happen* to drive future orders above the line. As such, although statistics have been applied to the data, executives cannot make any decisions from the charts on this dashboard; it merely reports a relationship between historical sales and profits.

AI-Enabled Analytics

To contrast mathematics as Informative vs. mathematics as Insightful, Figure 5.7 presents advanced analytics that combines correlations and statistical forecasts to triangulate on forecast accuracy of product units sold for Product SKU A. The bars to the left of the vertical dotted black line are the actual values of product units sold, and the bars to the right are a statistically calculated forecast for the next four months. The center line is a forecast calculated from a correlation with unemployment as a four-month leading indicator to product units sold, meaning unemployment four months prior is related to the current product units sold. Finally, the lines on either side of the center line forecast represent a statistical 95% probability that the actual outcome will fall between outer lines. The chart shows that the actual historical bars fall within these outer lines.

Comparing the historical bars with the center line shows a close relation between product units sold and unemployment (and represents a back-test) that leads to a level of confidence for using this correlated relation to forecast the next four months. This makes sense as the coefficient of correlation between units sold and unemployment (as a four-month lead indicator) is strong at negative 0.902 (as depicted by three cell bars). The negative value means there is an inverse relation; that is, as unemployment goes down, units sold goes up.

The forecast values of the bars and center line are almost the same for Sep 2019 to Nov 2019 but deviate from each other for Dec 2019, and this bar is also outside the upper line. When the forecast bars fall inside the outer lines, these are considered within a normal statistical variance. However, when a forecast bar is outside the lines, we considered that bar unreasonable, and the accuracy of the forecast value is to be questioned.

This example uses multiple advanced analytics to gain insights because we make decisions based on forecasts. Here, analytics warns us that Dec 2019 has a demand forecast that is questionable. Further action needs to be taken to home in on forecast accuracy before making decisions that affect downstream manufacturing, purchasing, and inventory.

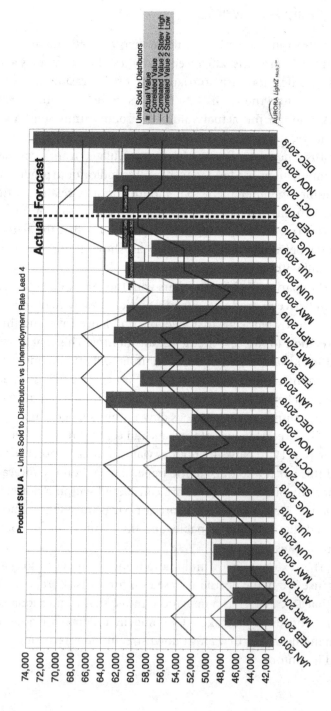

Figure 5.7 Forecast comparisons and reasonability test.

Toolbox and Persona

Previously in this chapter, we identified the categories of people skills as soft and hard and discussed the soft skills. Our focus will now turn to the hard skills. From our empirical research and experience, we have prepared Figure 5.8, which presents the average representative range of time to support an Analytics Culture across the tool types *Analytics, Data Visualization, Excel,* and *BI.* These are the hard skills as they are associated with the use of tools. Not surprisingly, Analytics (including desktop statistical and AI-enabled analytics tools) should be utilized 50% of the time, whereas Data Visualization is the next largest skill to provide operational information, report automation, and storytelling to executives. Excel is a material element of the landscape but should no longer be the dominant part of business. Finally, legacy BI is used for data-marts and some report automation.

People hard skills

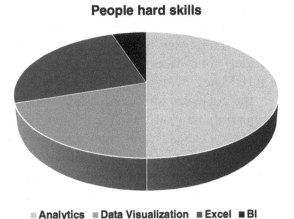

▨ **Analytics** ▨ **Data Visualization** ▪ **Excel** ▪ **BI**

Figure 5.8 Proportion of people hard-skill utilization in an Analytics Culture.

It is important to note that the tool does not make the Persona. For example, having an AI-enabled analytics tool does not make a Strategist unless the tool is used to find insights and make predictions that are used for decision-making. If the Analytics tool is simply to automate spreadsheet reports, then the Persona remains a Reporter.

Leveraging our empirical work, Table 5.1 further refines the utilization of tools to assign the average use for each associated Persona, with each Persona using some tools proportionally more than others. Tools also have practical characteristics in the size of data, the number of dimensions, and the application of arithmetic/mathematics. We refer to *practical* as what can be accomplished with data with a reasonable effort and response time for the user.

Not mentioned in the table is the level of skills or specialized skills required. For example, Excel can be used by all and is what we refer to as *self-serve*. However, BI tools are primarily maintained by IT and need specialized skills to program the cube (the BI database) and user reports. Some Data Visualization tools are self-serve as they sit on the desktop, while others need IT support to assemble and maintain the database. Desktop statistical tools are self-serve in that they do not need IT support, but you have to know mathematics and statistics to apply the requisite formulas on the data. Most AI-enabled analytics tools also require specialized skills for statistics and ML.

The Reporter primarily uses Excel with some BI to produce reports containing data and information that are accurate, timely, and accessible. The Reporter is not concerned with the efficiency of producing reports or the effectiveness of the reports to support decisions.

Moving up the Analytics Intelligence scale, the Commentator Persona uses primarily data visualization and Excel, with a bit of BI. Here, the Commentator can do report automation for more efficient report production and better information to contribute to decisions using multi-dimensional, multi-source data and larger data sets.

Insights begin with the Advisor, who engages all tools for reporting, report automation, data visualization, and analytics. The Advisor seeks to influence decisions with information and low-level analytics (like correlations) for insights, spending 60% of the time in analytics and visualization tools.

The highest level of Analytics Intelligence to gain insights and predictions is the Strategist Persona, who we gauge should spend about 70% of the time with AI-enabled analytics tools and the balance with Excel and data visualization (for storytelling to executives). The Strategist can do deep dives with AI-enabled analytics to impact strategic decisions.

Table 5.1 Persona, tools, and usage.

Persona	Tool	Tool primary classification	Tool characteristics	Tool proportional usage
Reporter	Excel (grey)	Informative	Small data sets / Small # dimensions / Simple analysis	
	BI (gold)	Informative	Large data sets / Medium # dimensions / Simple analysis	
Commentator	Data visualization (orange)	Informative	Large data sets / Large # dimensions / Simple analysis & analytics	
	Excel	Informative	Same as first above	
	BI	Informative	Same as first above	
Advisor	Desktop statistical (blue)	Insightful	Small data sets / Small # dimensions / Complex analytics	
	Data visualization	Informative	Same as first above	
	Excel	Informative	Same as first above	
	BI	Informative	Same as first above	
Strategist	AI-enabled analytics (blue)	Insightful	Large data sets / Large # dimensions / Complex analytics	
	Data visualization	Informative	Same as first above	
	Excel	Informative	Same as first above	

To be clear, our segmentation and proportions of tool usage are guidelines based on our empirical research and are not replete with hard boundaries. Further, each tool classification includes a range of tools to fit different uses and users. This is similar to, say, buying a car—there are many brands, models, colors, sizes, and trims. Analytics tools are no different.

For example, a department of a $3 billion technology company used two different analytics tools; four people liked one tool, and one person liked the other. The four people appreciated their tool for its intuitive use and automation, as it enabled them to be curious about the data rather than having to spend time manipulating the tool. However, the other person was clever and preferred their tool exactly because it required hands-on manipulation to make it useful. This did not make one tool better than the other—simply different, just as people are.

Yet too often, executives and/or policies require their organization to settle on one tool—which we refer to as *toolbox madness*. For example, the finance department of a major life insurance company wanted to employ analytics on its data and identified a software vendor to begin a POC. However, IT prevented the POC and restricted finance to the exceptionally large in-house analytics software used by its actuarial department, which required specialized statistical and programming skills.

The notion that analytics tools should be selected or managed by IT is a fool's errand. End-user tools are, well, for the end user. It is like a carpenter asking an electrician what woodworking lathe to buy. The electrician can provide the power to the outlet for the lathe but has no knowledge of how the lathe is used.

If IT drives the decision selection for analytics tools, the result will almost certainly be heartache. For example, the finance department of a Fortune 500 technology company tested an analytics tool that proved valuable for revenue quality management. However, IT said that it was developing an analytics tool and finance should not use external software. *Years* later, a pseudo-application was created, without much utility for finance. While there may be a light at the end of the tunnel that is not a train, many more years of work remain, on top of the years of work already spent, and finance is no closer to better revenue quality management.

To put an exclamation point on the problem of IT as the primary decision-maker for end-user tool selection, I was sitting with the IT director of a major cruise line, who said, "Our users are stupid! We give them all sorts of tools they don't use." In reality, the problem was IT providing tools users did not want or could not use.

Finally, while tools are a primary part of an Analytics Culture, they are *not* the end of building it. Too often, executives think that by having a tool, they are now AI-enabled to gain insights for data-driven decisions. This is a terribly wrong fantasy that always leads to wasted time and capital. Yes, analytics tools are the fulcrum for an Analytics Culture, but establishing the culture requires the requisite Mindset, People, and Processes to realize performance improvement from AI-enabled insights.

THE ROADMAP FOR IMPLEMENTING AI-ENABLED ANALYTICS

Note to executives: the Roadmap to an Analytics Culture is foremost a road of discipline: to start it, focus on it, stay on course, supply the needed resources, and benchmark progress.

This note should be printed, framed, and placed on your desk to remind you that by following these simple words, your analytics projects will be successful, and you will have built a culture of data-driven decisions that increase business performance.

With the components established for an Analytics Culture, we arrive at the Roadmap to it, as captured in Figure 5.9.[8]

In grand simplicity, the five axes relate the components of *Mindset, People, Processes,* and *Systems* with *Analytics Intelligence* and organizational *Personas*. The X-axis is *Mindset* to decisions. The left Y-axis is *Analytics Intelligence,* ranging from reporting data to deriving predictions from data. The right Y-axis is the *Systems* (tools) that yield *Analytics Intelligence*. The two Z-axes are *People* and *Process* for the remaining components to the culture of AI-enabled analytics. The figure's large central arrow represents the intersection of each *Persona* with the five axes.

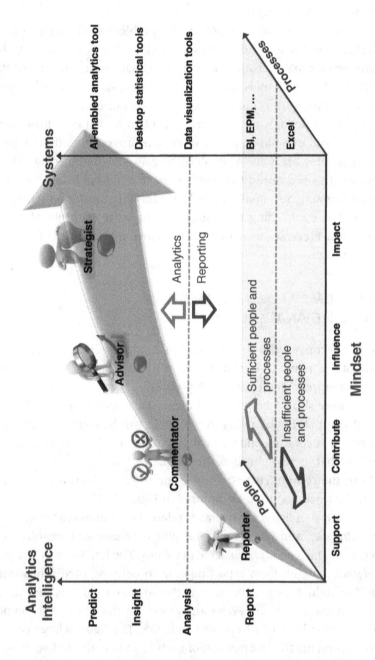

Figure 5.9 Roadmap to implementing analytics.

The Roadmap is a clear guide for your aspirational Persona. Once chosen, you simply extend the lines to each axis to know the associated Mindset, People, Processes, and Systems that achieve Analytics Intelligence. For example, to be a *Strategist* Persona requires the *Mindset* to *Impact* decisions and sufficient *People* with the requisite skills, along with written *Processes* of data and decision governance, which achieves the predictions of *Analytics Intelligence* from the *Systems* of AI-enabled analytics tools.

While it may seem that aspirations are a matter of personal choice, in today's and tomorrow's digital world, the only Persona an executive can practically choose is the Strategist. There could be an argument that not all executives need to be Strategists, but neither can any executive be less than an Advisor if their department, group, division, or company is to remain competitive.

However, most executives cannot quantify where they currently are on the Roadmap, which is why benchmarking is a critical activity. Benchmarks done by the Finance Analytics Institute reveal that most executives' organizations are somewhere between Reporter and Commentator; but when executives are asked before the benchmark, they often perceive themselves as Advisors or Strategists. As such, a benchmark is required to measure where you are compared to where you want to be and to quantify the soft/hard skills and toolbox gaps that must be filled to achieve the aspirational Persona.[9]

It is important to understand that each business area functions across Personas. For example, part of what manufacturing does is a simple Reporter of its production volumes by line. Managers want a Commentator to do variance analysis of each line's output year-over-year. Plant operators need insight from an Advisor whose analytics on process controller data is used for preventive maintenance. And executives need a Strategist to deliver unbiased predictions of long-range demand forecasts for decisions about manufacturing capacity and allocation for capital expenditures.

Note, too, the Z-axis with its dotted line in the sand to denote sufficiency: below the line, there are insufficient People or Processes to sustain an Analytics Culture. As in our discussion of Bobby in the basement, if the only person engaged in analytics is Bobby, then analytics will end when Bobby leaves. The same is true for Processes. If there is no Data Governance process, bad data is not resolved, and the garbage-in-garbage-out rule of bad data leading to bad predictions will apply. If there is no Decision Governance, analytics is just an exercise with no impact on the decision process.

Also note the horizontal line at the Commentator, which distinguishes between reporting and analytics; recall that data visualization and biased forecasts from a CRM system are not analytics (the application of mathematics on data to reveal insights). As we have discussed, data visualization can be useful but is often not insightful and certainly not derived from analytics.

To achieve an Analytics Culture, executives must ensure *focus*, *budget*, and *bandwidth*. When the CEO claims to want the business to be data-driven but distracts people by pulling them too frequently from one priority to the next, or makes no budget available for analytics tools and people training, or does not reorganize people's workload to make bandwidth available to integrate analytics into the business, then it is easy to see how quickly individuals will lose interest and drop the pursuit of an AI-enabled culture. This issue will be discussed extensively in Chapter 6.

The Roadmap and benchmark combine for every business of any size, providing instruction and visibility to become an analytics powerhouse that is competitively formidable and capable of making its future happen.

LAUNCHING THE CULTURE OF ANALYTICS

To strategically drive change, an executive must communicate the initiative to gain the desired behaviors. Leaders of analytics change must have a vision, articulate the vision, and motivate people to the vision, all of which can be wrapped in the message to achieve a culture of data-driven decisions with analytics.

This book gives clarity and voice to the Roadmap to the Analytics Culture, and now it needs to be reduced to strategic messages, whether you are a group leader, department manager, division head, or corporate executive. While each step in leadership scope becomes broader, the fundamentals of launching an Analytics Culture are the same and composed of three components: *Vision*, *Mission*, and *Roadmap*.

Vision has simplicity and clarity. For example, after the Soviet Union launched the Sputnik satellite, a space race was initiated. Then-President John F. Kennedy had a vision to *land a man on the moon.* Notice the specificity: Russia orbited a satellite, but the US was going to the moon. The US effectively said to the USSR, "I'll see your satellite and raise you the moon." More importantly, the vision was clear, concise, and delivered with confidence. For example, the Vision for analytics can be clearly articulated as *Enable data-driven decisions with analytics.*

A Mission statement needs to be self-actualizing; that is, it enables people to make decisions with minimum supervision. Kennedy expressed the mission to reach the moon as "This Nation should commit itself to achieving the goal, before this decade is out, of landing a man on the moon and returning him safely to earth." This is a most elegant Mission statement because it includes the goal (the Vision) and the key parameters that all involved with the goal must adhere to, as well as the time in which the goal is to be achieved.

All members of NASA were actualized to land a man—not a dog or robot—on the moon; to return him safely—not in pieces, as that would mean failure—and to accomplish the mission in less than 10 years. Similarly, the analytics Mission is to *Implement an Analytics Culture for data-driven decisions that yield insights to measurably and materially improve business performance within one year.*

A Roadmap is a route taken from where we are to our destination. For the moon shot, this meant going through a series of steps: from the single-man Mercury program that put one man in orbit, to the Gemini program that put two men in orbit, finally to the Saturn series three-man program that landed a man on the moon and returned him safely in 1969. Mission accomplished!

For analytics, we have the Roadmap to take us through the Reporter, Commentator, Advisor, and Strategist Personas. It puts forth the tools we need and the people, skills, and processes to achieve a culture of data-driven decisions with AI-enabled analytics. The Roadmap is progressive, and a benchmark is periodically employed to measure where we are and confirm that a portion of the Mission has measurably and materially improved business performance.

CONCLUSION

There is a joke in the project management of large engineering projects: "The good news is, we're ahead of schedule. The bad news is, we're lost." Without a tactical Roadmap for analytics, or without adhering to the Roadmap, expect to be ahead of schedule but lost in attaining the value from data-driven decisions. Executive support and leadership is the lynchpin to the success of the analytics journey, and discipline is the directive every leader must impose to ensure staying the course, remaining on the Roadmap, and achieving the intended benefits from the Analytics Culture.

NOTES

1. BrainyQuote. (n.d.). Winston Churchill quotes. (https://www.brainyquote.com/quotes/winston_churchill_124653).
2. Brandellero, M. (2020). Without Big Data, you are blind and deaf and in the middle of a freeway. LinkedIn. https://www.linkedin.com/pulse/without-big-data-you-blind-deaf-middle-freeway-moore-brandellero?articleId=6644603528507731968#:~:text=Today%2C%20companies%20are%20expected%20to,the%20middle%20of%20a%20freeway%E2%80%9D.
3. US Census Bureau. (2017). County business patterns. https://www.census.gov/data/tables/2017/econ/susb/2017-susb-annual.html.
4. Zwerling, R.J. and Sorensen, J.H. (2019). Mindset. Finance Analytics Institute, Analytics Academy.
5. Zwerling, R.J. and Sorensen, J.H. (2020). Automate, eliminate & elevate to gain bandwidth for analytics. Finance Analytics Institute, Analytics Academy.
6. Hans, J. (2017). Why Excel is a $60 billion black hole. RTInsights.com. https://www.rtinsights.com/why-excel-is-a-60-billion-black-hole.
7. Strategy@Risk. (2009). The risk of spreadsheet errors. http://www.strategy-at-risk.com/2009/03/03/the-risk-of-spreadsheet-errors.
8. Zwerling, R.J. and Sorensen, J.H. (2018). *Implementing an Analytics Culture for Data Driven Decisions*. Amazon.
9. Sorensen, J.H. and Zwerling, R.J. (2021). Temperature of finance 2021, assessing the finance journey to become an Analytics Business Partner. Finance Analytics Institute. www.fainstitute.com.

CHAPTER 6

Executive Responsibilities to Implement Analytics

The greatest leader is not necessarily the one who does the greatest things. He is the one that gets the people to do the greatest things.

—Ronald Reagan[1]

Executives must recognize the importance of aligning analytics with key processes as well as institutionalizing cultural and organizational shifts. Implementing AI and advanced analytics in their organization is a requirement to improve operating performance, stay competitive, serve customers, and satisfy stakeholder expectations.

In a recent McKinsey global survey on digital transformation, "eight out of every 10 respondents said their organizations have embarked on a digital transformation journey in the last five years. That is promising news. However, only one third of these initiatives have succeeded. For such organizations, the digital transformation journey remains elusive."[2]

According to McKinsey, this can be solved by looking "outside" when evaluating "people, process, data, and technologies." But companies will not succeed if they view these components separately rather than being integrated and aligned as expressed in the Roadmap.

In building the Analytics Culture, leadership cannot be outsourced to consultants, as no matter how experienced, they are not part of the corporate legacy and are not accountable for the business strategy. While outside consultants should be part of the implementation process, reliance on them to drive the culture is fraught with peril.

The critical factor to analytics success is the executive's mindset that assures the organization shares the same aspiration. It is the executive who can make or break the implementation of achieving an Analytics Culture by their lack of support to engage, train, and equip. It is the executive who aligns the organization and drives people to develop the culture that ultimately determines success; no amount of outside resources can replace the executive and the people.

According to a separate McKinsey study, "successful organizations. . . *think* differently about AI. At these companies, AI is etched in the collective mindset. Having this mindset means deeply internalizing the long-term competitive benefits of augmenting human decision making."[3]

So how do we establish the internal mechanisms to manage the implementation effort? How do we devote the right resources and best practices from within our organization? More importantly, how do we identify areas needing attention and devise actions to mitigate and enhance our AI-enabled capabilities and achieve the potential from AI and analytics?

The framework for implementation resides in executive oversight in three key areas that we will discuss: (i) Executive Commitment, (ii) Analytics Champion, and (ii) Change Management.

EXECUTIVE COMMITMENT

The road to AI-enabled analytics and the ability to implement an Analytics Culture for data-driven decisions *must have* executive engagement and approval. Without buy-in from executives, it will not get attention, nor will it get funding. But executives are often the biggest obstacle for implementing an Analytics Culture simply because they do not have the Roadmap or are not keenly aware of the benefits analytics can bring to the organization.

Many executives knowingly or unknowingly contribute to a failed implementation by not having, or not listening to, or not developing their analytics thought leader. Further, executives often fail to understand the backbone components of Analytics Culture of Mindset, People, Processes, and Systems. But even more important, if you do not get to this level of understanding soon, you are at risk of being sidelined as other executives step up their analytics game and adopt AI-enabled analytics.

There are three primary pillars of executive commitment: *budget, bandwidth,* and *focus*. Executives need to be keenly aware of what these commitments entail to assure they are not the cause of analytics derailments.

Budget

Budget encompasses hiring and training people, building the software toolbox, and developing data and decision governance processes.

While executives naturally lean toward hiring people, especially for analytics, they often resist training existing personnel in analytics or replacing staff who lack the requisite skills to support analytics. This is not to say executives do not want to train existing staff, but to highlight that this training reflects the needs of the current culture vs. training geared toward achieving the new Analytics Culture.

Then too, there is a propensity to "cheap" the toolbox and constrict the tools needed for analytics or just "make do" with what they have. Finally, executives almost always fail to engage outside consulting help to build the critical data and decision governance processes to institutionalize the Analytics Culture. The belief that internal staff can somehow find a material amount of time to build the requisite processes is misplaced.

During the budget allocation process, executives need to recognize the balance between maintaining current levels of performance and future resources required to drive the adoption of the Analytics Culture. This chasm can always be bridged through the resulting ROI from analytics and should not impede the allocation of resources.

Bandwidth

The concept of bandwidth relates to people having the time to adopt and maintain an Analytics Culture. When people's days are already full, the task of implementing a new culture is mitigated or precluded simply because there is no time available—and analytics projects then "die" from neglect. When approaching bandwidth, the executive must consider reducing unnecessary work that can be accomplished by eliminating low-value and redundant activities and automating routine, repetitive tasks.

Focus

Executives need to keep their organization focused on the completion of the implementation of an Analytics Culture and must recognize they are often the chief culprit to the prevention of analytics taking root. Executive misdirection originates in the form of "fire drills" and reprioritization:

■ *Fire drills* come in many "sizes and flavors." For example, when an executive requests a task that is interpreted by the organization as "Stop what you're doing and focus on my task" vs. continuing the efforts needed to implement analytics, routine work stops to ensure completing the task's deliverables on time. Once the task is complete, the organization has to play catch-up before returning to the analytics implementation. Weeks can go by before people finally ask, "Where did we leave off?" and more time is wasted before analytics can resume.

■ *Reprioritization* occurs when the executive routinely changes the emphasis for what people should be actively working on and the timeframe to complete it. If analytics is a priority today but tomorrow the priority is something else, people lose commitment to implementing analytics. They lose focus when priorities change too frequently, so much so that analytics becomes lost in the wind.

There are indeed times when distractions are warranted and required, such as natural disasters, regulatory non-compliance, and disruptive competitive threats. But these are sporadic occurrences that everyone can understand and will not undermine the overall implementation, as they are seen as only temporary disturbances.

ANALYTICS CHAMPION

Executives do not have the time or technical expertise to drive the detailed implementation of analytics and, as such, need an *Analytics Champion* who has the time and talent to manage a project of this scope and importance. The executive assigns and actively supports an Analytics Champion who *directly* reports to the executive, shares the executive's vision, and is given a mandate to manage the implementation.

The Champion needs a basic level of analytics knowledge that includes the ability to distinguish data visualization from AI-enabled analytics and arithmetic from mathematics, and some experience with the use of analytics tools.

The Analytics Champion's role is to manage the analytics project and enable the executive to primarily understand, commit, and motivate the organization to the framework—that is, the Roadmap—of how to build an Analytics Culture (Mindset, People, Processes, and Systems).

The Analytics Champion provides regular reports and feedback to the executive on the project's progress. The executive can utilize a matrix or direct line organizational approach to the Analytics Champion. Either can work, and the approach that is more compatible with the organization's culture, structure, HR practices, and policies should be selected.

We have included as an appendix the Analytics Champion Framework, which is a detailed guide for the Analytics Champion and includes four major areas: (i) qualifications for selecting the AC, (ii) ground rules the AC and executive must adhere to, (iii) skillsets the AC must develop, and (iv) details to starting and managing an analytics project.

In concert with the Analytics Champion, the executive must periodically obtain a benchmark that quantifies the progress toward completing the analytics Roadmap and measuring benefits for business performance improvement from AI-enabled analytics. One such benchmark, from the Finance Analytics Institute (FAI), effectively gauges and numerically presents advancement and current position on the Roadmap to the executive's aspirational Persona.

Figure 6.1 is an excerpt from the FAI benchmark report for a particular company, measuring its Analytics Culture Index on the Y-axis on a scale from 0–100, with 0 being no culture and 100 perfectly fulfilling each component of culture (Mindset, People, Processes, and Systems) on the X-axis. Also shown are dotted lines representing comparable peer companies' scores in the top and lower quartile and a dashed line for of the median score.

The triangles depict the company's *baseline*: that is, its current state as measured by the benchmark survey. The squares project the company's *target* state: its aspiration. A company's target can be set by comparing its desired level of performance to a designated peer group. Once the difference between the baseline and target is revealed, a *gap analysis* results, from which an implementation plan is prepared to achieve the aspiration. The Roadmap described in Chapter 5 enables an organization to develop a gap-closing implementation plan.

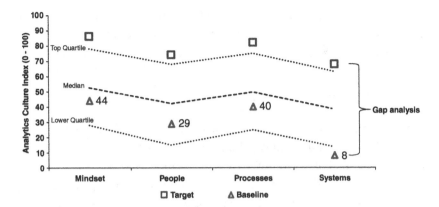

Figure 6.1 Analytics culture readiness.

In this case, the company's aspiration was to be in the top quartile, but its Mindset, People, and Processes were located between the median and lower quartile, and the Systems component fell below the lower quartile. This single chart marks the critical importance of the benchmark, as if you do not know where you are today—baseline—and understand where your peers operate, then it is difficult to have a competitive aspiration—target—for where you want to be and know how to fill the gaps to get there.

CHANGE MANAGEMENT

Ultimately, organizations will need to adopt AI and analytics for data-driven decisions. The Analytics Champion must elevate the importance of organizational change management and collaboration to enact the Analytics Culture for data-driven decisions.

There are many sources of information on leading change to ensure the organization has devoted the right technical and business competencies and sufficient resources and, where necessary, arranged to involve individual(s) to manage the change management program.[4] A change management leadership role requires an understanding of the broader social and behavioral issues involved in implementing innovations and new ways of working.

Several characteristics, most of which are present and easily accessed, can be used to effectively facilitate change and include *communications, collaboration, culture influences,* and *behaviors and recognition.*

Communications

Frequent and informative communications are essential to effectively introduce an AI analytical capability to the organization. Generally, a communications plan supports messages and activities conveyed with already established media vehicles, such as a company newsletter, e-mail announcements, and success stories posted on internal web pages.[5] What is important is that the organization is informed about how the process contributes to operating results and tangible benefits, as well as the WIFM (what's in it for me).

Establish a strong presence and understanding among managers and staff regarding why, what, and how analytics can contribute to the success of the business. Peer sessions and one-on-ones with key players are mechanisms to convey the narrative about why we are doing this, what we hope to accomplish, and how we are pursuing the end results.

Collaboration

In a collaborative organization, clear accountabilities and the interdependence of various departments or divisions are linked to business events and their anticipated outcomes, thus rendering a more cohesive understanding of organizational impacts. Managerial actions and intended results are continuously shared and respected, and the organization's ability to learn and disseminate critical knowledge to other areas is advanced and trusted. There is clear buy-in of the analytics Roadmap and a strong sense of leadership and executive support for actions and decisions that drive improvements and optimize performance.

Cultural Influences

Culture influences and shapes our acceptance of risk in different ways. The managerial act to postpone a decision reduces the risk and possibly the embarrassment of making a mistake, but it can also mean missing an opportunity. Both involve risks.

By better understanding cultural influences on behavior, executives and senior managers striving to successfully deploy analytics may better succeed and avoid roadblocks that might derail these initiatives.

Being aware of your company's cultural influences will have a direct impact on the likelihood of success and represent an important opportunity to adhere to the implementation Roadmap.

Behaviors and Recognition

The adage "You get what you measure" holds true with business analytics. Therefore, driving desired behaviors and results requires leaders to develop, align, and measure key metrics within the executive's organization for the desired outcomes. Rewards and recognition might be used to foster behaviors of the organization, such as innovation, teamwork, and collaboration. The organization should use rewards and recognition to promote risk-taking actions that have been approved to promote the Analytics Culture.

CONCLUSION

We started this chapter by referencing a McKinsey global survey that shows a mere one-third of digital transformation initiatives have succeeded. McKinsey's conclusion was to involve outside resources to manage the transformation. However, as we have put forth in detail, based on distinguished research and empirical experience, an Analytics Culture is built from the inside. It is the executive who has the critical impact on whether an analytics initiative will fail or succeed. The executive must (i) commit to supporting the requisite budget, bandwidth, and focus for the people in the organization; (ii) assign an Analytics Champion who will be responsible for managing the implementation of the Analytics Culture; and (iii) ensure the necessary change management.

NOTES

1. AZ Quotes. (n.d.). Ronald Reagan quotes. https://www.azquotes.com/author/ 12140-Ronald_Reagan.
2. McKinsey. (2018). Unlocking success in digital transformations.
3. McKinsey. (2021). Winning with AI is a state of mind.
4. Kotter, J.P. (1996). *Leading Change*. Harvard Business School Press.
5. Adapted from Maisel, L.S. and Cokins, G. (2014). *Predictive Business Analytics*. John Wiley & Sons, Inc.

CHAPTER **7**

Implementing Analytics

Tell me and I forget. Teach me and I remember. Involve me and I learn.

—Benjamin Franklin[1]

With executive commitment to budget, bandwidth, and focus and the Analytics Champion in place, an organization is ready to launch an analytics project toward becoming an analytics powerhouse. As depicted in Figure 7.1, the organization moves through five steps: (i) defining a problem, (ii) selecting an AI and analytics software vendor for a proof of concept (POC), (iii) performing the POC, (iv) benchmarking people's skillsets, and (v) scaling analytics with learnings from the POC across the executive's span of authority.

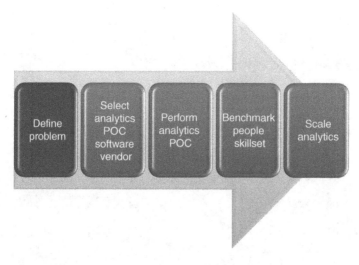

Figure 7.1 Five steps to implementing analytics.

DEFINE THE PROBLEM

Many organizations incorrectly start their analytics project by spending months and months—often with a consultant—setting a vision, mission, and strategy; defining processes; etc. But no insights are found that executives can use for data-driven decisions.

Instead, the organization would be better served with the Analytics Champion working with the department leaders who can quickly identify and prioritize problems that analytics is suited to solve. Note that "problems" can be in many flavors and can include optimizing a process (e.g. budgeting, forecasting, long-range planning, etc.) or accelerating a growth opportunity (e.g. price increase, new product introduction, etc.).

As we have discussed, analytics has a broad range of applications, and there are many places to begin defining the problem. For example, manufacturing wants to reduce unplanned maintenance, or brand managers want to increase sales while minimizing promotions, or finance needs better revenue quality management for cash flow, and so on. The key here is that we are seeking to find solutions or optimizations, which is the wheelhouse of AI and analytics vs. plain reporting data.

For a major health insurance company, the POC began by defining how to improve profits. But the company recognized that *profits* by itself was an overly broad term to encompass the entire business; and after all, this was a POC. The process to crystallize the problem was enlightening because it is transportable to any business.

The problem must be large enough to have material benefit yet small enough for a POC. The area of a small group (SG) was chosen as it balanced size and materiality. A SG was defined as an employer that has from 2 to 50 employees. The question followed regarding profitability vs. number of employees, which revealed that an employer with two employees could be profitable as long as the employees, considered as a group, were healthy (i.e. making fewer claims). The health of the group was more important than the raw number of employees when driving profitability, but a bigger healthy group also generated more profit.

After several more iterations of questions, the problem was pinpointed to the size of the employer's group, the health of the group, and whether the employer would churn (i.e. not renew its contract). Churn was further refined to predict whether it would happen six months in advance so the insurance company would have time to take action to retain the employer. As such, the profitability of the SG could be improved if larger employers with a healthy group could be retained. The POC problem definition was *Find those larger size (25 to 50 employees) Small Group customers that have the top two health ratings with a predicted propensity to churn in six months.*

SELECT AN ANALYTICS SOFTWARE POC VENDOR

Attention now turns to finding an analytics vendor to solve the identified problem. Selecting the AI-enabled analytics tool is managed by the Analytics Champion, who ensures that the tool meet five minimum business requirements:

- Cost-effective
- Easy to use
- Speed to value
- Efficient to solve the business problem
- Understandable analytics to business users

For *cost-effective*, the selected software should be capable of use by existing POC users without the need to hire specialized skills. If the software needs data scientists and the POC users are not data scientists, the software is not cost-effective, as it will require the added cost burden to retain this skill.

Easy to use is assessed by the POC users in their sole judgment. However, *speed to value* has a guideline: in our experience, roughly 30 days should suffice for the POC because the focus will be to back-test predictions, and doing so should be relatively swift. If it takes more than 60 days to prove the analytics software's capability, the POC is too large/complex or the software is too large/complex.

The final two bullet points, *efficient to solve the business problem* and *understandable analytics* (to the POC) business users, are related. The former means the user has a modicum of control over the analytics software to attain the insights sought. If the software needs technical intermediaries to translate user requirements to configure/program the software, it is not efficient. The latter point is related to the previous one: if the analytics software requires intermediaries to translate what the output means for POC business users, the analytics output by itself is not understandable.

Most analytics vendors will run a POC free of charge without having the organization commit to up-front investments in software, hardware, data scientists, and other resources.

A common mistake when launching an analytics POC is the assumption that this is an IT project, and IT must approve new software. While IT should be part of the process, it should *never* be the department defining which tool to use or usurp the Analytics Champion's responsibility to manage the software selection.

The CIO should not be the gatekeeper in vendor selection because the CIO will not be a user of the analytics software sought by the business. The CIO does have a role in the policies, priorities, and practices of IT that include software support and data security. But the Analytics Champion must challenge a CIO's desire to limit the software to in-house tools or tools favored by the CIO that are unacceptable to the users.

The Analytics Champion must steer the identification, evaluation, and selection process of analytics vendors. When a conflict arises between the CIO/IT and the Analytics Champion in making the software choice, the sponsoring executive must support the Analytics Champion.

PERFORM THE ANALYTICS POC

The POC starts from the defined problem that then triggers the discussion about the data to be used and analytics to be applied on the data that make predictions and/or forecasts to back-test for confirmation of accuracy. Historical data is readily available and will be largely of sufficient quality to perform the test. It has been our experience that early in the test, data quality is readily identified and deficiencies corrected.

A guideline for the time frame of a POC is 30 days, plus/minus two weeks. Tests that take three to six months often involve other technical resources, coding, and IT support. Tests that reach this size and duration typically become paid pilot projects and not the free lightweight POC.

It is not uncommon for an organization to do a POC, obtain good results, and then, instead of proceeding to a roll-out, do a pilot.

This is a measured approach that costs more time and money, but the slow pace enables the organization to have more flexibility to adapt to the changes that an analytics will bring.

When doing predictive analytics, some remarkable results can be obtained, and executives must not let their biased thinking intrude on unbiased insights. For example, an executive at a major recycling company was interested in whether the trend and price of cardboard waste could be forecast six months in advance within 10% of the actual price. A POC proved this achievable, but the executive simply would not accept the results, saying, "The truth is, I can't make myself believe this works."

As discussed in Chapter 2, this is an example of how System 1 thinking can cause us to question outcomes or results that are seemingly counterintuitive to our experience or belief. However, these outcomes are derived from analytical techniques, and executives must learn to trust the science and not their gut.

The POC has three important guidelines concerning data, benefits, and impediments. First, data is not always perfectly accurate! No surprise here, but do not fret, as perfect data is not a prerequisite; simply having a sufficient amount of data that is sufficiently accurate will do. The measure of sufficiency will become apparent as the POC progresses. As such, do not be alarmed about data difficulties, as all that is needed is to methodically work through it. The efforts will be rewarded with better data and better data governance.

Second, benefits must be measurable against a performance target that is set in the Define Problem phase. If the POC results in only qualitative benefits, then the POC has failed, and you need to find a quantifiable benefit or begin again with a new problem that has a measurable performance target. For example, if the POC results in happier employees because they are doing data analytics vs. data compilation, this may cause them to stay longer with the company. But unless there is some quantification of the benefit of employee retention, the POC has insufficiently proved its value.

Finally, the POC reveals important data, processes, and organizational impediments to scaling analytics across the organization. Here too, there is no need for panic, as impediments should be welcomed learnings: their resolution will lead to lower cost, higher value, and lower-risk scaling effort. For example, it is common to expose that current staff has technical skills deficiencies in using analytics tools. This is normal, as analytics is often the new kid on the block; and as long as people have the requisite soft skills (as discussed in Chapter 5), the hard skills of learning a new tool can be taught. Knowing the required level and scope of training in advance will lead to better training and setting realistic capabilities expectations for a smoother scaling of analytics.

BENCHMARK PEOPLE SKILLSET

After a successful analytics POC, it is necessary to assess if people with the requisite skills are available to meet the future requirements for aspirational Analytics Intelligence. Organizations must benchmark people's skillsets to determine if they are sufficient to generate insightful findings. These skills are related not to data science and programming but rather to analytical thinking and a curiosity to uncover insights from data.

In benchmarking, the first step is to establish a baseline, then compare it to the analytics skills required, and then calculate a gap analysis of the difference. The baseline can be assessed using surveys or interviews or by shadowing assigned tasks. Although interviews and shadowing are good for assessing the current state, they are not quantitative. As such, it is a best practice to do a survey to reveal the current state and measure the gaps to the aspiration, which will be used to develop a plan to close the gaps. The importance of benchmarking cannot be ignored, because if you do not know where you are, you cannot chart a course to where you want to go.

With benchmark in hand, the executive has several options to close the gap, including (i) training internal people, (ii) hiring external people, and/or (iii) outsourcing analytics to a third party. Training internal employees has advantages for employees who feel motivated and more engaged by advancing their skillsets. The advantage of hiring an external skillset is quick onboarding of the required skills, but these resources suffer from a lack of understanding of the business operation and a trusted relationship with the business.

Analytics outsourcing is an excellent option for companies that do not have personnel with the right skillset and do not want to hire additional headcount. Outsourcing sends data to an external group with the skillset and toolbox to perform analytics and deliver insights. This option has advantages of speed to engage analytics and deliver advanced insights without investing in software, hardware, and expensive specialized headcount.

SCALE ANALYTICS

After a successful implementation of an AI-enabled analytics POC and developing the right skillsets, the next step is to scale the analytics to other departments. The learnings from the POC will instruct the next implementation, which will be iteratively more efficient.

Even after a successful POC with multiple back-tests, some executives may remain doubtful about adopting analytics in their organizations. In this case, the Analytics Champion can work with executives to find a mutual path to incorporating analytics. For example, a Fortune 100 company was struggling with quarterly forecast accuracy from the Sales organization. The Finance group stepped in and developed statistical forecasting that, in back-tests, proved to materially increase accuracy. However, before the executives were ready to adopt analytics, they wanted Finance to show three consecutive quarters of better forecast accuracy versus the roll-up forecast from the Sales organization. With three quarters in a row of significantly better forecast accuracy, the executives agreed to utilize the analytics forecast from Finance.

The Analytics Champion may encounter departments that are resistant to change, and the sponsoring executive must intervene to lead change, as described in Chapter 6. One method to mitigate resistance in advance is for the executive to advocate for an analytics initiative by sponsoring the Analytics Champion to make presentations at executive leadership team meetings on the progress and benefits achieved from the analytics project.

Scaling incorporates learnings that can be applied to other departments. For example, in Chapter 4, analytics was used to reveal the characteristics of a sales path that led to a high, medium, or low propensity for a sales deal to close. A similar technique can be applied by HR in recruiting new hires to determine the characteristics of candidates who have a high, medium, or low propensity to excel in the position and become a top talent.

ILLUSTRATIVE EXAMPLE OF THE ANALYTICS POC

This example illustrates a basic approach to implementing the POC and begins with asking the fundamental question of what we are concerned about: in other words, what is the problem that needs to be solved? This is the first step in the process of *Systematic Thinking*™, a proven method to perform analytics projects developed by the Finance Analytics Institute.

Systematic Thinking "is a methodology to analyze data by assembling it in a *logical hierarchy* and applying *unbiased analytics* to yield *insights*." The components of Systematic Thinking are as follows:

- Define a Question (a problem or goal).
- Develop a Hypothesis (an answer to the Question).
- Collect Data (needed for the answer).
- Apply Mathematics (used to answer the Question).
- Organize Dimensions (hierarchical filters used to segment the Data).

Let us create a fictitious company, Electronics-R-Us, that manufactures business and consumer electronics sold through distributors that are retailers. John is the executive heading sales for the Business Solutions division. He is concerned that recent sales are less than budget and wants to introduce AI and analytics to gain insights that can improve sales performance. John selects his director of sales, Billy, to be his Analytics Champion, and asks, "How can we improve the trend in stores?"

Billy is a curious man, so he replies, "Which trends and stores are you interested in?" A discussion ensues in which each man challenges the other with questions that probe into crystallizing the problem—in this case, the goal to be attained. They arrived at the question, "How can the trend of gross sales of each product in each of our distributor (retailer) stores be improved?"

With the question determined, Systematic Thinking follows to hypothesize an answer. In this case, Billy believes sales trends can be improved by taking advantage of the opportunity about current good trends that AI predicts can get better and focusing brand managers to fix bad trends that AI predicts will further deteriorate.

Following from the Question and Hypothesis comes the definition of Data, Mathematics, and Dimensions that will be needed. Specifically, the Data and Dimensions include point-of-sale data over the past two years at each retailer store for each SKU. The software vendor will determine the application of mathematics that can be used (and back-tested) for trend predictions.

Billy selects an AI-enabled analytics vendor that will do a free POC. Also, since AI trend prediction analytics is sophisticated and Billy has no data scientists on his team, the software chosen does not need statistics or machine learning skills or IT support.

The POC begins with each distributor (city) store and each SKU, to learn its year-to-date trend, and the AI prediction of the future of the trend, a sample of which is depicted in Figure 7.2. The variance analysis of the Monitor 19 product for each distributor displays the trend (positive values are up and negative values in parenthesis are down) and the last right-hand column predicts (with an arrow) the future trend direction. Together, these illuminate several important points.

AURORA *LightZ* Mach 2™ PREDICTIONS	2019 YTD	2018 YTD	YTD Variance	YTD % Variance	12 Months Predicted Trend Direction	
Fry's_Denver_Monitor 19	2,061,325	2,018,753	42,572	2.11% ⬆		0.69
Fry's_Philadelphia_Monitor 19	2,247,731	2,172,996	74,735	3.44% ⬆		0.79
Fry's_Phoenix_Monitor 19	2,078,486	1,815,644	262,842	14.48% ⬆		1.28
Fry's_Seattle_Monitor 19	2,411,130	2,319,263	91,867	3.96% ⬈		0.18
Inacom_Phoenix_Monitor 19	4,892,687	5,540,940	(648,253)	(11.70)% ⬆		0.43
MicroAge_Los Angeles_Monitor 19	5,365,389	5,967,233	(601,844)	(10.09)% ⬇		(0.38)
MicroAge_Philadelphia_Monitor 19	5,247,233	5,915,232	(667,999)	(11.29)% ⬆		0.78
MicroAge_San Diego_Monitor 19	4,702,322	5,422,729	(720,407)	(13.28)% ⬇		(0.44)
MicroAge_San Fran._Monitor 19	4,213,008	4,726,503	(513,495)	(10.86)% ➡		0.09
MicroAge_Seattle_Monitor 19	5,770,724	6,899,897	(1,129,173)	(16.37)% ⬆		1.45
MicroAge_St. Louis_Monitor 19	4,566,831	5,044,578	(477,747)	(9.47)% ⬇		(0.29)
Monitor 19	43,556,866	47,843,768	(4,286,902)	(8.96)% ⬆		0.35

Figure 7.2 Trend and predicted trend direction.

First, without the predicted trend, managers would ignore the good (positive) trends (as these are not broken) and concentrate on the bad (negative) trends to fix. However, the trend prediction pinpoints bad trends that are predicted to improve (e.g. Inacom_Phoenix_Monitor 19): that is, a bad trend that is already on the mend. In this case, managers need not spend their limited time on items in recovery and instead focus on the bad trends predicted to get worse (e.g. MicroAge_Los Angeles_Monitor 19), as these are truly broken. Second are the good trends predicted to get better (e.g. Fry's_Phoenix_Monitor 19). These are opportunities for Electronics-R-Us to direct its sales force to work with the distributor to increase the price and/or add volume. Third, using built-in predictions with the arrow icon to indicate the future trend direction makes the predictions easily understood by the Analytic Champion without the need for onboarding data science skills or having IT support.

In this example, we see how analysis and AI analytics combine to produce insights that change decisions that (i) focus managers on the SKUs and stores that need fixing and not have their time consumed on areas that are already moving toward repair, and (ii) take advantage of unseen opportunities to increase revenue. These actions combine to achieve the goal of improving the gross sales trends in distributors' stores for each of the manufacturer's products.

With a successful POC, the Analytics Champion has a showcase to roll out to the other business units and scale analytics. The scope can expand to, say, find supply-chain disconnects between the manufacturer and distributor stores, efficiency analysis for product portfolio management to improve operating profit, correlations to find leading indicators of demand for each product at each distributor store, and so on. As more is done, the overall revenue and profits of the company and the company's customers will increase.

ANALYTICS POWERHOUSE

The analytics powerhouse is achieved when the Roadmap of AI-enabled analytics for data-driven decisions is implemented, as represented by a majority of departments under the executive's responsibility. For example, if the executive is the CFO and has tax, audit, controller, and FP&A, the powerhouse is attained when decisions through the departments are broadly derived from the application of AI-enabled analytics.

The Analytics Champion will have to deal with boulders that will arise to resist scaling, such as changing major processes driven by spreadsheets, people who lack confidence in their ability to learn new tools, dealing with the spotlight that analytics can shine, arguments about data quality, turf wars as to who owns the decision-making authority, and so on.

We can now see with clarity the importance of the executive and Analytics Champion to drive the organization to become an analytics powerhouse. Together they understand the company and its strategy, complexity, ambiguity, and interplay of the internal environment.

CONCLUSION

The path to becoming an analytics powerhouse is straightforward, from internally identifying a problem to solve to selecting an analytics software vendor and completing a successful POC. With success in hand, people skills can then be benchmarked, and the results of the POC become the showcase to scale analytics to a majority of departments. All this, however, is fundamentally dependent on the executive's commitment of budget for analytics, the bandwidth of the people to incorporate analytics, and focus on maintaining the discipline to complete the installation of the Analytics Culture. Essential to the executive's success is the Analytics Champion, and essential to the Champion's success is the support of the executive.

NOTE

1. BrainyQuote. (n.d.). Benjamin Franklin quotes. https://www.brainyquote.com/quotes/benjamin_franklin_383997.

CHAPTER 8

The Role of Analytics in Strategic Decisions

All men can see these tactics whereby I conquer, but what none can see is the strategy out of which victory is evolved.

—Sun Tzu[1]

AI and analytics should play a governing role in strategic decisions; but, sadly, executives too often employ gut feelings, refer to a single case example, or simply make a decision up front. Yes, we have all done this, but using our learnings from Chapter 2 in biased decision-making, now is the time to recognize how we trick ourselves or fall prey to our passions or the politics of the moment.

We are human—no getting around that—and with 4.5 billion years of evolution wired into us, we will be hard-pressed to ignore our tendencies. Our biggest driver is gut feel. We simply react to our environment. For example, in the book *The Righteous Mind: Why Good People Are Divided by Politics and Religion*, by Jonathan Haidt (published by Gildan Media, LLC), there is an elucidating discussion of our decisions on morality, which Haidt describes as an "elephant and rider" where we are the rider. We decide what is moral from an almost unconscious perspective based on many factors (e.g. culture, politics, etc.). We are likened to being a rider on an elephant: only with great effort do we alter its course. However, we perceive that our moral decisions come from our high-and-mighty thoughts driven by fairness and refined by intellect—and we are mistaken!

OK, so we are not the towering moral beings we may perceive ourselves to be, but surely, in business, our environment gives us rational thought—doesn't it? Well, not always. Even here, what we determine our reality to be is not necessarily true, and we often fool ourselves to shortcut the decision process. As such, let us first discuss how we can "trick" ourselves into decisions and how tactical decisions can affect strategy. Then we will explore the applications of analytics for determining the value drivers of our organization and the innovative concept of an Analytics Scorecard for building sound and sustainable strategy.

HOW WE TRICK OURSELVES

Strategic decisions are hard because, well, they are strategic. But gut feel, using a single case example to prove a point, or making a decision up front suffocates a thoughtful decision process. For example, a CFO for a $500 million CPG company had the gut feeling that his distributors were driven to purchase the manufacturer's products based on the distributor's sales to the distributor's customers (the retailers). However, an analytics correlation between sales from the manufacturer to the distributor and distributor to retailer showed no relation that one was driving the other.

The CFO was dumbfounded with this finding, as it seemed to defy his sense of what business should be. Recall from Chapter 2 that the CFO engaged in *inherent bias* by having a plausible theory for what was happening that relied on his assumption (gut feel) or association of what he thought should happen.

In this case, analytics revealed to the CFO that distributors were holding millions of dollars of the manufacturer's product in inventory but seemingly did not care about the cost of holding inventory. In fact, distributors knew they had excess product tied up in inventory, but that did not affect their purchasing decisions. Distributors were driven by the price at which the manufacturer's products could be bought, and when considering gross profit, the distributor's inventory carrying cost was discounted or disregarded. For the distributor, if it could get a $2 product for $1.50, that was all that mattered; so it over-bought when the manufacturer promoted its products and just held the products in inventory.

Another of our tendencies is the *single case* justification where we remember one event that happened that is like what we are considering, and we use the past to justify that it will happen again—but one point doesn't make a trend! This is almost as bad as when we have already decided (for whatever reason) and then command our staff to justify it. Both these modes of decision-making are fraught with peril because of the lack of discipline, objectivity, and rigor.

These modes to make decisions often lead to under-optimized or bad strategic decisions, and the first step on the road to redemption is to recognize when we are working from the gut or a single example, or deciding before investigating. Especially if the decision is strategic, we should ensure that AI and analytics are an integral part of the process. If this seems obvious, then why is this not the rule?

Unfortunately, the higher up in the company and the more strategic the decision, the more politics dominates the process; and politics is about self-interest. There, we said it! Politics is intertwined in most human decisions. And although it cannot be prevented, it can be managed through analytics.

TACTICS THAT AFFECT STRATEGY

Most organizations struggle to keep operational tactics aligned to their strategy, as it is easy to lose sight of goals when in the weeds of everyday business. This is compounded by our biases, which infect our decisions. Let us explore two typical tactical activities that can have a material impact on corporate strategy—*sandbagging* and *the big ego*— and discuss the application of analytics to mitigate bias.

Sandbagging

Everyone has been in a situation where the sales forecast seems a bit off. The executive—say, the CFO—has a "feeling" that the Sales or Marketing organization is too conservative when forecasting revenue. But the feeling is not enough to reverse a forecast, especially when the CFO does not have sufficient knowledge to challenge any deal in the forecast. As such, the business is left over-performing in revenue.

While over-performing may sound good, especially when bonuses are based on performance, the consequence is potentially under-performing on revenue. Suppose 10% more revenue was possible with the existing resources. What about 20% with added headcount? This is exactly what happens in an international engineering company every year, as sales reps, once they meet their quota, hold back closing sales toward the end of the year (to drift to the next year) in an effort to get a jump on sales for the new year.

The remedy for quota setting and driving sales performance is an AI forecast with a Monte Carlo simulation. The AI will deliver an unbiased forecast based on past performance (managed by the sales reps);

however, Monte Carlo will present a range of probable forecasts. Here, management can ask for a higher forecast to the top part of the first confidence interval (as discussed in Chapter 4). This target is higher than the sales sandbag forecast but statistically probable and, as such, reasonable. Over time, this will drive sales rep performance continuously higher, even with sales rep manipulations.

This also plays out the other way: that is, when more revenue is being demanded by management than can be reasonably provided. For example, a vice president of sales of the western region of a manufacturing company was asked for 5% more sales. The VP was distraught, as his region was struggling to meet the current target, let alone increase sales. Was the VP just sandbagging?

A statistical forecast of the region showed, with existing resources, a year-over-year decline. If new headcount was added, it would be insufficient to materially change the outcome for the balance of the year. The VP rejoiced in the analytics that confirmed his concern about the unreasonable demand to achieve a sales increase.

These examples, while tactical, have a significant strategic impact: in particular, on the company's valuation. For a public or private company that is contemplating a merger or acquisition, getting the forecast consistently right and driving steady growth is what drives valuation higher.

The Big Ego

Ready? We executives have big egos. No surprise, as the meek and shy do not seek the executive limelight. However, we often lead with our ego to expand our responsibility without necessarily considering if that is best for the entire company. Sub-optimized operations lead to lower performance, but introducing analytics can pave the way to better results.

For example, the shipping executive of a $300 million distribution company wanted to add more headcount to load more distribution trucks faster—an admirable goal. However, the CFO "felt" that more headcount was not the solution and proceeded to do an efficiency analysis of the truck loaders.

Using data from the shipping and time-keeping systems, a database was assembled from each loader and each truck type the loader loaded, and the data was input into software to run efficiency calculations. Each week the number of cubes (palettes of products) loaded by each loader into each truck type (ranging from a step-van to an 18-wheeler) were tracked. The efficiency of cubes per week by loader was calculated by truck type (a step-van has a small capacity and is hand-loaded, whereas an 18-wheeler has a large capacity and is loaded with a forklift).

The results of the measure of efficiency of each loader by truck type were posted in the warehouse for all to see. The loader with the highest efficiency across all truck types was recognized with their picture on the wall, and management worked with loaders in the bottom quintile to find ways to improve their performance. Over time, loaders as a group and individually became more efficient, as the top loaders wanted to stay on top and the laggards strove to improve.

Within a year, performance had increased so much that there was no need for more loader headcount, even with increased distribution volume. This tactical example can have a strategic impact during long-term capital planning to decide whether to invest in a material handling system that can support growth in distribution volume.

KEY PERFORMANCE INDICATORS (KPIs) AND STRATEGIC OBJECTIVES

Analytics is integral to an organization's *key performance indicators (KPIs)* and *strategic objectives*. The former is a measurable element that drives performance to optimize the result. The latter are the underlying objectives that guide the KPIs. For example, KPIs include a telecom company focused on customer churn, meaning how to maintain its existing subscribers; an oil and gas company focused on how to get the most oil from the ground by optimizing its yield per drill; or a SaaS (software) company focused on new bookings, meaning how many new customers it can add to its current contract base; and so on.

KPIs are straightforward for each business, but strategic objectives can be challenging to define. For example, customer churn is the KPI, but why does a customer churn? Customer satisfaction, price, the solar eclipse? Interestingly, a report by CGMA and Oracle, *The Digital Finance Imperative: Measure and Manage What Matters Next*, found that the top five strategic objectives (what they referred to as *Value Drivers*) across all industries are customer satisfaction, quality of the business process, customer relationship, quality of people, and brand reputation.[2]

However, these strategic objectives, at a high level, are qualitative and assumptive. It is through the application of analytics that objectives can be confirmed and quantified, like correlations between customer satisfaction and customer churn might reveal a relationship. Analytics can further reveal the exact customer satisfaction rating or *breakpoint* that defines whether a customer will or will not churn. Being able to link KPIs and their corresponding objectives enables executives to make decisions based on the analytics on data and not feelings about the drivers of the business.

For example, a car manufacturer wanted to know which of its incentives were driving retail sales. A correlation identified dealer rebates as related, but only in the second half of the year. Upon learning this correlation, the marketing executive jumped to his feet and declared, "I knew it! The dealers are pocketing the dealer rebate in the first half of the year to build their profits and using it in the back half to clear old inventory to make room for the new year's models!"

Without analytics, the company was shelling out incentive money inefficiently. With analytics, the company could cut in half the incentive in the first half of the year and double it in the second half, which would balance the dealer's financial satisfaction with the manufacturer's goal to sell more cars.

THE ANALYTICS SCORECARD™

Many years ago, a group of us (KPMG consultants and company executives) collaborated to develop the Balanced Scorecard (BSC) approach.[3] Balanced Scorecard, KPI reporting, or any driver-based approach is designed to assist management in measuring performance and improve decision-making. The framework was intended to help executives clarify their company's strategy and use the scorecard for three primary purposes: (i) measure and manage strategy execution, (ii) communicate strategy to employees and other stakeholders, and (iii) align resources and encourage cohesive organizational behaviors and decision making.

As depicted in Figure 8.1, BSC follows a common method for a fictitious telecom company, PhoneCalls-R-Us, which starts with developing an agreed-on strategy map among executive leadership. The map articulates the strategic theme (e.g. top-line growth) with its associated KPI (e.g. Customer Churn), strategic objectives (e.g. Increase Customer Satisfaction), and their relation to each other with lines with arrows to identify the cause-and-effect relation between strategic objectives.

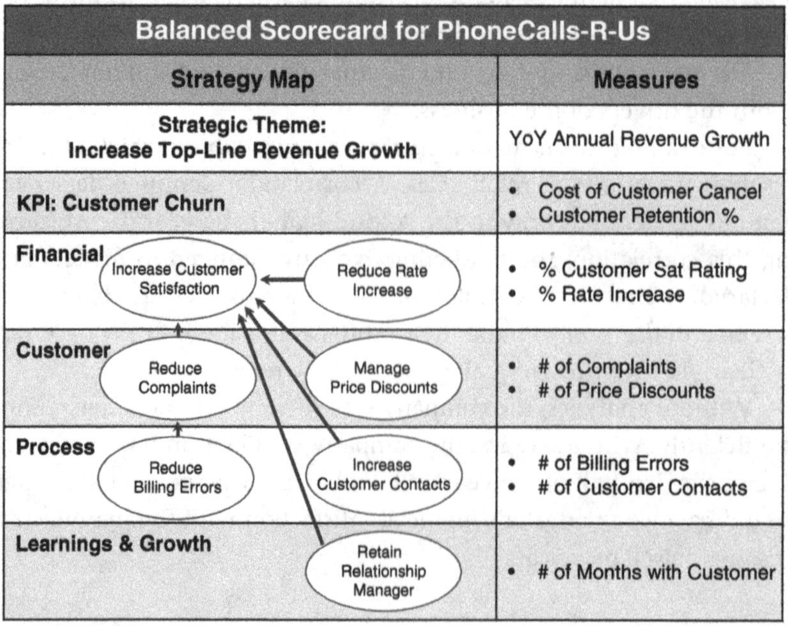

Figure 8.1 BSC for PhoneCalls-R-Us.

Alongside the strategy map are the measures for each KPI and strategic objective. BSC also goes further to set target values for each measure, fund improvement initiatives, and report progress at quarterly executive strategy review meetings.

Many companies and organizations have adopted BSC to effectively manage strategy, but BSC has a significant flaw that materially limits its effectiveness: the KPIs, strategic objectives, and cause-and-effect relations linking strategic objectives are subjectively derived from interviews and workshops with operational management. While management has a view of what may affect performance, they have not mathematically determined if such relations exist. Specifically, neither the strength of the relation nor the threshold of each strategic objective affects on related objective(s) and the KPI.

While operational managers are savvy about their business, they are not always correct about the cause-and-effect relations that drive the business, as we demonstrated earlier with the CFO who incorrectly assumed that distributor sales to retailers were directly driving purchases of the CFO's products. Even when managers are correct, they may overestimate the strength of the relation and increase costs inappropriately, like the example of the VP of Distribution who wanted to increase headcount to increase distribution volume instead of improving the efficiency of existing headcount.

This flaw exists in BSC because it was developed years before AI and analytics were available at scale to dive deep into large data sets to identify and quantify strategic objectives, KPIs, and the relationships to the strategic theme. As such, we have developed a groundbreaking *Analytics Scorecard (ASC)* to complement the BSC and make BSC far more effective in translating strategy into actions based on data-driven decisions. The four key innovative components of the ASC are as follows:

- *Identify & Validate* the strategic objectives and KPIs along with cause-and-effect relations
- *Strength & Direction* of the relation
- *Threshold* to establish the value at which the relation is valid
- *Impact* to measure the lower relation effect on its upper relation

Identify & Validate determines quantitatively if a strategic objective and KPI exist and their relation: e.g. does the KPI of customer churn really affect revenue, and is customer satisfaction correlated with customer churn?

Strength & Direction measures the strength of the relation and the direction in which it operates: e.g. customer satisfaction is strongly correlated with customer churn and is inversely related directionally, so customer churn decreases as customer satisfaction increases.

Threshold determines the point at which the relation is valid: e.g. suppose the threshold to impact churn is when customer satisfaction is above 80%; as such, a 5% rise in customer satisfaction from, say, 70% to 75%, will not produce a decrease in churn.

Impact calculates the improvement the lower strategic objective has on its related upper strategic objective or KPI: e.g. a 5% rise in customer satisfaction above the threshold of 80% produces a 4% decrease in customer churn.

Figure 8.2 shows the Analytics Scorecard for PhoneCalls-R-Us and its integration with and improvement of the BSC. At each dimension (e.g. Financial), the ASC defines and determines whether each strategic objective (e.g. Reduce Rate Increase) is linked with the KPI (Customer Churn) and then cascades to each of the other strategic objectives. Analytics identified that the strategic objective, # of Recent Price Discounts, does not have a cause-and-effect relation with its higher dimension of Increase Customer Satisfaction. As such, in the ASC, the former objective is shown in dark grey to denote no relation, and the line-and-arrow connection is removed.

Most interesting in the ASC is the inclusion of a new strategic objective, # Recent Store Visits, which was found while doing analytics on the data set. Although this objective was not initially looked for or known, analytics revealed that it was related to Increasing Customer Satisfaction if the customer made three or more visits to the retail store in the last 12 months (LTM) before the end of the term of the contract.

Accordingly, ASC redraws the strategy map to critically find what is and what is not a strategic objective. Knowing this enables a data-driven decision to focus on customer satisfaction and not give away revenue in discounts as a fruitless effort to stem customer churn.

The Analytics Scorecard is essential to the BSC as the ASC (i) applies *unbiased* statistical methods to quantify the cause-and-effect relationship among measures, while the BSC relies on subjective management judgment that, although informed, is assumptively bias; (ii) calculates analytical values of the relationships to provide insights that can be used to develop plans for improvement; (iii) is unbounded by organizational structure and functional silos; and (iv) has analytics capacity to dive deep beyond second- and third-order effects among

Analytics Scorecard for PhoneCalls-R-Us

Balanced Revised			Analytics		
Strategy Map	Measures	Identify & Validate	Strength & Direction	Threshold	Impact
Strategic Theme: Increase Top-Line Revenue Growth	YoY Annual Revenue Growth				
KPI: Customer Churn					
Reduce Rate Increase	• Rev of Customer Cancel	✓ Cancel impacts rev growth	✓ High & Inverse	✓ None	✓ 1:1
	• Customer Retention %	✓ Retain impacts rev growth	✓ High & Inverse	✓ None	✓ 1:1
Financial — Increase Customer Satisfaction	• % Customer Sat Rating	✓ Cust Sat correlated w/churn	✓ High & Inverse	✓ >80%	✓ 1:1
Increase Store Visits / Price Discounts	• % Rate Increase	✓ Rate increase correlated	✓ Med & Inverse	✓ >5%	✓ 1:0.05
Customer — Reduce Complaints	• # of Complaints	✓ Complaints correlated	✓ High & Inverse	✓ >3 LTM	✓ 1:1
	○ # of Price Discounts	○ Price Discount not correlated	○ NA	○ NA	○ NA
	• # of Recent Store Visits	✓ Store Visit correlated	✓ Low & Direct	✓ >3 LTM	✓ 1:1
Process — Increase Customer Contacts / Reduce Billing Errors	• # of Billing Errors	✓ Bill Errors correlated	✓ Low & Direct	✓ >2 LTM	✓ 1:0.005
	• # of Customer Contacts	✓ Customer Contacts correlated	✓ Med & Direct	✓ >4 LTM	✓ 1:0.005
Learnings & Growth — Retain Relationship Manager	• # of Months with Customer	✓ # Months w/Cust correlated	✓ Low & Direct	✓ >3 LTM	✓ 1:0.005

Figure 8.2 Analytics Scorecard.

strategic objectives to quantify the relative impact on the KPI and pinpoint operational areas for improvement.

The ASC powerfully informs the tactical initiatives to meet the strategic theme. For example, to get a 2% increase in annual revenue growth requires a corresponding 2% reduction in customer churn (because of the analytically determined one-to-one relation). To accomplish the improvement in churn, the ASC identifies seven cause-and-effect relations of strategic objectives that will reduce churn. Management will decide which objective(s) to employ to affect churn based on their cost-benefit and time-deployment assessments of approaches.

The ASC is a beautiful advancement arising from the availability of modern AI and analytics. Further, it need not have a BSC as a starting point. Any driver-based map, like the KPI report or Six Sigma, that has biased assumptive cause-and-effect relationships is ripe for applying the Analytics Scorecard. The ASC delivers an incredible advancement to enable management to transform what they thought to be their strategy into a true quantifiable strategy for action using unbiased AI-enabled analytics.

CONCLUSION

Analytics comes in various forms that help the executive's dialogue, judgment, and ability to make better decisions. When business acumen is aligned with analytics findings, better decisions are made versus just trusting in human intuition and gut feelings, single case examples, or decisions made up front. By applying analytics and finding the connection between business drivers and the underlying value driver, executives can understand where to focus and know the impact of a change in a value driver on the business driver.

NOTES

1. BrainyQuote. (n.d.). Sun Tzu quotes. https://www.brainyquote.com/quotes/sun_tzu_155751.
2. Chartered Global Management Accountants and Oracle. (2015). The digital finance imperative: measure and manage what matters next. https://www.cgma.org/content/dam/cgma/resources/reports/documents/the-digital-finance-imperative-report.pdf.
3. Nolan, Norton and KPMG, a Corporate Consortium. (1986). The balanced scorecard approach.

PART III

Use Cases

CHAPTER 9

Cases of Analytics Failures from Deviation to the Roadmap

Do not be embarrassed by your failures, learn from them and start again.

—Richard Branson[1]

This portion of the book is extraordinarily enlightening, especially in terms of why analytics fails to get traction even in the face of successful pilots. We will see how failures are obvious and avoidable yet happen for the most flawed reasons. It is a tragedy to have achieved successful proofs of concept (POCs) that are then discarded for the worst of excuses. When the gold ring is in hand, it is lost—not dropped clumsily but wantonly thrown to the ground. It is a shameful loss of time and capital when business performance improvement has been proven and then is not pursued.

However, with budget, bandwidth, and the discipline of focus, the fruits of an AI-enabled Analytics Culture for data-driven decisions are immense. We will discuss reachable projects with exceptional results in manageable time frames.

The worst-case scenario for implementing analytics is the loss of a modicum of time and capital, which is not a threat to the business. But an existential threat to the business results from being blind to insights due to the lack of analytics, as it leaves you unaware of competitive threats, market opportunities, and broken internal processes. The cases to be discussed were all achievable with discipline, budget, and focus that almost any company can afford and that yielded insights to better plan the future rather than react when the future arrives.

Sadly, many AI and analytics POCs or pilot projects, even when successful, fail to be implemented, typically due to deviation from the Roadmap. Executives are the central characters in the success of building the Analytics Culture but are more likely to cause its delay or failure. Fortunately, executive-induced failure is self-inflicted and thus avoidable. As there is much more to be learned from failure than success, the following three areas of Roadmap derailment emphasize the most common pitfalls when implementing an Analytics Culture:

- Failure due to mindset commitment
- Failure due to insufficient people and processes
- Failure due to toolbox confusion

The examples include the gaming, grocery, technology, and telecom industries. While you may be in a different industry, *these examples are completely transferrable* because the failures are due to deviation from the Roadmap and are independent of the industry.

MINDSET COMMITMENT

A major Las Vegas resort sought to experiment with improving its slot operations with analytics of data (beyond spreadsheets), with the goal of determining how to get slot machine players to play more. Slot player activity was tracked through loyalty cards. Players were rewarded through compensation (comp) in the form of complimentary meals, drinks, cigars, hotel rooms, etc. The more a player played, the more comp they received.

A pilot project was commissioned to gain insights on (i) how to retain slot players and (ii) how to increase play. This led to determining how to quantify the following:

- A *Value (Slot) Player*
- Retaining a Value Player's *Loyalty*

Although a slot player may take the time to apply for a loyalty card, simple performance analysis on the data found that most players played only once. While this was intuitively known, the quantitative reality was much larger than expected, and it had a material cost impact. In particular, all slot players were marketed with a variety of mailers year-round regardless of their level or frequency of play. Instead of carpet-bombing all players with mailers, the casino would do better to solely target its Value Players.

As such, a Value Player was established through a series of calculations that incorporated such elements as volume and frequency of play vs. costs to market and support the player while at the casino. Next, a further statistical calculation was used to establish Loyalty, meaning a player who would continue returning to the casino to play. The analytics also had the added benefit of identifying a player's lifecycle.

Just like a product's lifecycle, a player has a beginning (growing play), middle (plateau of play), and end (declining play) at the property. Eventually, players tire and leave for a variety of reasons;

but by knowing where players are in their lifecycle, the casino can gain insight to encourage more play and extend the player's lifecycle by giving a better experience. While there was a qualitative feel for where a player might be in his lifecycle, there was no unbiased quantitative predictive methodology, and thus players were not proactively managed.

Player Loyalty ultimately came down to the level of comp, which could be calculated as a percent of play, known as *Theo Win* or the Theoretical Win. This value of Theo Win is the amount of money the player is calculated to lose to the casino (that is, the casino's win) based on the money input into the slot machines.

The percent of comp to achieve the player's Loyalty was an insight because of the amount and the fact that it was the same percentage regardless of Theo Win: that is, a player whose Theo Win was $100 and a player with $1,000 required the same percent of comp to retain Loyalty.

Accordingly, analytics of comp across players revealed that too much comp was going to too many lower Theo Win Value Players, while many higher Theo Win Value Players were getting less than the comp percent needed to retain their loyalty. By simply rebalancing comp among players, play could be increased for the higher Value Players without having to spend more money on comp across all players and without losing the Loyalty of lower-Value Players.

Along with several other analytics, the pilot found that slot revenue could have increased an average of 6%, had the pilot been implemented. However, rather than being implemented into operations, the pilot simply ended, as the executive over slots had no interest in analytics regardless of the return. The executive believed a good slot manager operated by knowing the business and not analyzing the business. For him, experience trumped mathematics, which he saw as a waste of time. The pilot was merely an exercise to satisfy senior executives who had the notion of employing analytics.

From the onset, the results of the pilot were to be irrelevant, as the Mindset to incorporate analytics in operations never existed. This is a breakdown of the worst kind because there was no commitment, and the capital of the casino and the time of the software vendor were wasted in a fruitless exercise.

So, how did the slot executive get away with ignoring the results? It turned out that the 2008 recession that devastated Las Vegas was the cover to curtail spending on any new systems.

There was a further missed opportunity in this story. As the data was already available, the pilot took the opportunity to perform a statistical forecast on casino revenue nine months hence and projected a material downturn. The executive laughed at this forecast, understandably, as there had not been a downturn in Las Vegas gaming. Nine months later, an analyst at the casino lamented that if they had only listened to the analytics, they might have taken mitigating action ahead of time.

INSUFFICIENT PEOPLE AND PROCESSES

A $1 billion regional retail and wholesale grocer had the Mindset to improve forecasting for its retail chain stores by incorporating statistical forecasting into its monthly planning processes. Its goal was to increase average weekly sales forecast accuracy across stores to 98% over 52 weeks and cut the labor of its monthly planning process by 50%. With these well-defined goals, a software vendor was selected, an Analytics Champion from finance assigned, and a project begun.

In an astounding six weeks, the software for forecasting and reporting was built, installed on the company's servers, and successfully back-tested for 52-week accuracy. Data sources were identified, data pull routines were prepared, the finance leader was trained on the software, modification to planning procedures were identified, and demonstrations were given to key people as a prelude to roll-out.

Everything was ready to go, when the company began an organizational realignment that delayed implementation of the roll-out for eight weeks, after which the finance Analytics Champion was promoted to a new position. The Champion's replacement had no knowledge of the software or the targeted high-value goals sought from analytics. He was simply overwhelmed in his new position.

The replacement was not prepared to roll out a project he had no familiarity with, and there were no processes in place to ensure continuity of the hand-off. As such, the software vendor assessed the need for a restart in training the new finance leader to cover the project goal, software, and framework for the processes that needed to be developed.

The software vendor offered to cover most of the cost of the effort with a modest $10,000 increase in budget. The new finance leader supported the revised budget to management, but the executive in charge decided to be penny wise and pound foolish. To avoid spending the added $10,000, the executive abandoned the $100,000 investment in the analytics project and the achievement of the company's goals. A billion-dollar company that prefers a one-time $10,000 cost avoidance over achieving its targeted performance improvement is what the fictional character Forest Gump might refer to as "Stupid is as stupid does."

With only one man trained and no procedures, it became a case of Bobby-in-the-basement; and when Bobby was gone, so was the opportunity for analytics. The situation was completely avoidable, but the road to failure was chosen. The last word, "chosen," is the most important. *Building the culture of analytics is a discipline, but its failure is often a choice.*

TOOLBOX CONFUSION

Next to Mindset, toolbox confusion on the Roadmap is the next big killer of building an AI-enabled Analytics Culture. The most common failure is to not sufficiently build the toolbox: that is, primarily using spreadsheets and/or severely limiting the number of other tools. What follows are three common examples of toolbox constriction: *Good Enough Is Good Enough, Just Hire More,* and *It's One & Done,* where executives confuse software cost with value, ignore software for people, and see all software as the same, respectively.

Good Enough Is Good Enough involves executive inaction that often stems from complacency with the status quo in small to mid-sized companies and fear to derail a career in large companies. As an example of complacency, I recall sitting with the president of a small CPG manufacturing company and showing him how to attain better demand forecast accuracy with statistical forecasting. He asked how much the software would cost. My salesman responded, "If it can better your bottom line by $2 million a year, what would you be willing to pay?" The president tersely replied, "I wouldn't spend more than

$5,000 on any software!" With that statement, we shook hands and ended the meeting.

This example typifies the attitude of *Good Enough Is Good Enough*: my business is fine the way it is, and I do not need to spend any more money on anything else to make more revenue or profit. Here, the executive is focused on maintaining the status quo.

If the issue is negotiating a price, that is one thing; but discarding the prospect to materially improve the business is cutting off the nose to spite the face. However, what if the president did not believe that increased forecast accuracy could be had? In such a case, he need only challenge the vendor to run a back-test POC. But he did none of this and just went about his business.

As an example regarding career derailment, I sat with a supply-chain executive of a Fortune 500 technology company who had just experienced a significant failure to predict demand, which resulted in too much inventory sitting with distributors. Using AI-enabled analytics, a back-test showed that unbiased predictive signals were available to sound the alarm at least six months prior and alert demand planners to a downturn in demand.

The executive listened to the presentation, saying nothing for 30 minutes. I then stopped to ask if he had any questions, to which he replied, "No." I responded, "If I'm wasting your time, let's stop here." A dialogue ensued, and we finally came to the crux of the issue: while he believed that analytics could be of value, he did not want to go out on a limb and be the first to use it and risk it not working. Having his team use spreadsheets would suffice until another executive took the risk to first prove the value of analytics.

In large companies, many executives achieve their positions with a political astuteness that complements their talents in business and communications. However, the politics of being associated with a failure can and often do cause a blind eye to innovation, even when such innovation can have material benefits, because an executive could be painted with that failure. As such, being risk-averse is the preferred path to advancing one's career.

Just Hire More is the most common toolbox failure: the organization simply refuses to expand its toolbox and elects to hire more people. The typical attitude is to keep using Excel and hire more Excel jockeys.

The notion is that the business will get more from more people using spreadsheets than by acquiring a tool to automate spreadsheet reports and provide analytics insights.

This is often seen in growth companies, as their view regarding many issues is to just hire more people. For example, a division in a major regional healthcare provider was expanding, and the FP&A group was determining how to handle the anticipated growth. Although the FP&A manager expressed a desire to use analytics to gain productivity and better information, in the end, she just hired more people to accomplish the expanded spreadsheet reporting. It was easier to go with more staff doing more of what they had been doing than to use analytics to gain speed and insights with the existing staff.

It's One & Done is the other most common method of strangling the toolbox by limiting the number of tools to one. For example, an agency of the Canadian government sought to employ analytics for better planning in support of its new integrated business plan. They did a successful POC with an advanced AI-enabled analytics tool and began the procurement process, only to be told by IT to standardize on the data visualization software already in-house.

Now, it would have been one thing if the two software tools were relatively similar, but they were not. It was like a car vs. a truck. Both are automotive transports, but with different purposes and markets. Here, both tools were different and had different emphases: one was primarily used for data visualization, and the other was specifically designed for AI-enabled analytics on business data. The moral of the story is that using one tool may achieve standardization, but it will not necessarily get the job done right.

CONCLUSION

AI-enabled analytics failures outnumber successes not because of technology, but due to the lack of a Roadmap or disconnects on the Roadmap. As we have stated, AI and analytics are not hard, long, or expensive—they are disciplined.

Mindset, People, Processes, and Systems are the components of the tactical Roadmap to implement an Analytics Culture of data-driven decisions. Learn from the lessons of failure, and benchmark yourself on the road to success.

Welcome to the future of business! It will have AI-enabled analytics as part of augmenting human judgment in making decisions and managing operations. Choose to wait at your own peril when others will not. Once thought safe, white-collar jobs will be lost, but the replacements will be new white-collar jobs filled with men and women who have curiosity. And after all, it is the intellectual pursuit of curiosity that sets humans apart from all other animals and artificial intelligence.

These cases are transportable to any industry and company of any size. The failures are more illustrative and informative because in analytics, it is easier to succeed than to fail; and the examples show how avoidable failure is. *Failure is a choice, so why do it? Success is a discipline, so why wait?*

NOTE

1. BrainyQuote. (n.d.). Richard Branson quotes. https://www.brainyquote.com/quotes/richard_branson_452112.

CHAPTER 10

Use Case: Grabbing Defeat from the Jaws of Victory

T his use case is based on a restaurant and bar located in Southern California[1] prior to the government-ordered shut-down of hospitality locations in response to COVID-19. Kent Bearden was vice president of operations for the Saint Marc USA restaurant chain. He was responsible for managing all restaurant operations including design and construction of restaurants, compliance, public relations, financial planning, and forecasting. Each restaurant had a general manager and two assistant managers who oversaw procurement, supplier relationships, media, marketing, and staff scheduling.

Kent is a food and beverage industry veteran with 20 years of experience in senior and executive positions with Breakthru Beverage (a major wine and spirits distributor), signature restaurants including Carmine's of New York City, Danny Meyer's Blue Smoke, Shake Shack (an industry leader in the use of analytics for operations), and the MGM Grand Hotel Las Vegas (where he pioneered the use of data for better purchasing of wines and spirits across some two-dozen bars and restaurants on the property).

Kent believed that Saint Marc USA was underperforming its potential. In particular, its onsite managers made too many operational decisions based on their prior industry experiences and gut feel. Kent wanted to demonstrate that improvements could be achieved by combining data-driven analytics with industry experience. As such, he embarked on an analytics pilot at one of the restaurants with three key goals:

Goal 1—Optimize store staffing to better align anticipated customers within each day and meal period to the number of wait staff needed to meet customer service standards and gain efficiencies (to mitigate the impact from upcoming mandatory minimum wage increases).

Goal 2—Increase forecast accuracy of liquor demand, especially regarding whether to take advantage of volume price discounts offered by vendors.

Goal 3—Find insights not specifically being sought.

So, what were the reasons for each goal? First, Kent noted that general managers make decisions about operations using gut feel, and it is common to "solve problems by throwing too much staff at it."

Kent was concerned that managers scheduled more staff than optimal, which, while assuring customer service, reduced profits.

Second, the bar drove 52% of revenues. To decide whether to accept a vendor's wine or liquor discount program when offered, managers merely used a snapshot of past consumption without any unbiased analytical predictions to help them know if they were making a good decision.

Third, Kent simply asked, "What else we could find from the data?" to gain that "Aha!" moment. With current systems, it was too hard to explore data to gain opportunities to improve performance, and the hope was that analytics tools could facilitate this discovery.

Kent had leading industry software, including Oracle Micros point-of-sale (POS) system, as well as Excel. However, the POS was labor-intensive and required gathering data and then using spreadsheets to assemble reports that were error-prone. This was "one reason we needed more staff in each location."

The POS system essentially gave only a fragmented data dump that required staff to spend two hours each day entering data in spreadsheets and working in the back office to produce various reports required for purchase planning and staff scheduling. Kent lamented that he asked managers to do low-IQ report compilation while paying them to do high-IQ operations and planning management. Kent found assistant managers preferred to "hide in the back and peck away at the keyboard."

While the POS did have a variety of attractive data visualizations, these were not particularly helpful for operational decisions. And although there was analysis, the POS essentially had no analytics or AI.

Accordingly, Kent began a proof-of-concept (POC) test with an AI/analytics software company to evaluate whether AI-enabled analytics could be applied to his chain to increase performance. Data from the POS system would be loaded and extensive back-tests conducted to assess achieving the goals. Further, Kent selected the vendor because the software offered intuitive AI and analytics, built-in automated reporting, charting, and forecasting that would alleviate the manual spreadsheet compilations and deliver deep insights "without a major investment and without the need of IT and data scientists."

POC RESULTS—REALIZING THE THREE GOALS

The POC enabled Kent to assess each of his three goals to provide information on scheduling, insights on liquor vendor volume discounts/pricing, and find unknown insights that could optimize performance. Additionally, the AI-enabled tool increased the speed and ease of reporting, eliminated much of the low-IQ report compilation, and increased operational visibility such that Kent could reduce one assistant manager at each location.

Goal 1—Optimize Store Staffing—Balance Customer Service vs. Labor Cost

Each restaurant needed to anticipate its customer volume to plan and schedule staffing:

- *Guess* staffing too high: service is great but with reduced profits
- *Guess* too low: service suffers but with higher profits and lower revenues
- *Guess* right: optimize customer service along with revenues and profits

But how to know what was right in advance? One approach was to calculate a detailed sales efficiency ratio, Sales Per Headcount, for each meal period for each day of the week, as depicted in Figure 10.1.

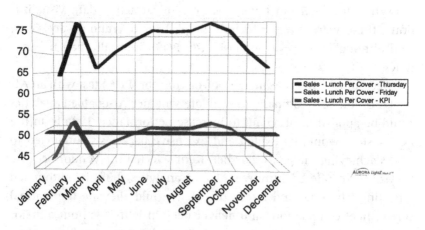

Figure 10.1 Sales efficiency KPI.

The horizontal line is the target key performance indicator (KPI) for the desired operational efficiency (total revenues $ divided by total # of covers for each meal period for each day of the week). The chart compares the actual sales efficiency by day by meal period against the target KPI, and according to Kent, "It is the inherent value of the guest that we are trying to optimize at the location." Above the horizontal line, they were understaffed and more efficient; and below the horizontal line, they were over-staffed and less efficient. In either case, lack of optimization impacted revenue, profit, and guest experience.

The lower line visualizes Friday at the lunch meal period and shows that the restaurant was overstaffed relative to the KPI target, which contradicted the manager's gut feel that Friday was the day of the week with a busy lunch and after-work period (time to socialize). In reality, special events and team meetings were held by local companies on Thursday, and people would socialize at the bar after work more often on Thursday. Thus, the manager should revise the staffing schedule to have more staff for Thursday vs. Friday. The upper line confirmed the Thursday lunch meal period as understaffed against the KPI: a true "Aha!" moment for the location since they were seeking to optimize staff scheduling.

As a result, Kent increased profits by changing staffing to better align the restaurant's busy times and achieved cost savings without lowering service quality or diminishing brand reputation.

Goal 2—Increase Forecast Accuracy of Liquor Demand

Liquor sales were the most profitable part of the restaurant, and volume-based liquor discounts from vendors were an attractive tool to increase profits. For example, suppose a tequila vendor offers a 20% discount on five cases (60 bottles) if the restaurant takes delivery this week. Is this a good deal? It depends on demand:

- *Guess* demand is too high: capital is tied up in excess inventory.
- *Guess* too low: lose the discount, which would have been additive to profits.

Store managers guessed demand based on how they *felt* sales had been: if liquor sales had a good week, the manager would say yes to the discount, and if not, the answer was no. Figure 10.2 presents a report for three tequila products displaying: (i) YTD sales, (ii) YoY trend variance, (iii) AI-calculated 12-month predicted trend direction, and (iv) number of months trend up (down) of the last consecutive trend.

AURORA LightZ Mach 2™	2017 YTD	2016 YTD	YTD Variance	YTD % Variance	12 Months Predicted Trend Direction	Number of Months Trend Up (Down)
TEQUILA						
Patron Silver 750ml	15,298	17,603	(2,305)	(13.10)% ⬇	(0.89) ⬇	(3)
Don Julio Silver 750ml	13,274	13,803	(529)	(3.83)% ⬇	(0.49) ⬇	(3)
Ocho Silver 750ml	12,546	13,503	(957)	(7.08)% ⬆	(0.14) ⬆	1

Figure 10.2 Tequila products report.

Focusing on Patron Silver 750 ml, we are informed with clarity that the YTD trend (as expressed by the variance) is down 13.1% and the number of months trend up (down) has been down for the last three consecutive months. Most important is the 12-month predicted trend direction, which displays an arrow showing AI prediction that the future of the trend is downward. Here we have an informative bad trend as expressed by the arithmetic variance, which is predicted to decline further as expressed by the downward arrow derived from the application of AI and analytics. That's insight!

The information and insights contained in the report conflicted with the general manager's gut feel. Clearly, unbiased analysis/analytics did not support the decision to accept the Patron distributor salesman's offer. To further confirm this decision, a separate AI forecast of unit sales for the next three months, as seen in the report of Figure 10.3, confirmed the downward AI-predicted trend indicator for Patron Silver 750 ml to be 14 cases less than the same three-month period of the prior year.

AURORA LightZ Mach 2™	Tequila 3 Month Forecast – Jan to Mar 2018			
	2017	2018	2017 vs. 2018 Variance	2017 vs. 2018 % Variance
TEQUILA				
Patron Silver 750ml	3,754	3,740	(14)	(0.38)%
Don Julio Silver 750ml	3,266	3,255	(11)	(0.33)%
Ocho Silver 750ml	3,041	3,013	(28)	(0.92)%

Figure 10.3 AI-calculated three-month forecast.

Using AI and analytics changed decisions to turn the tables: that is, the move to target purchasing, where the objective was to seek out the distributor rather than wait for the distributor to come forward with a discount. As Kent said, "In essence, we are smarter than they are," and he could get better discounts sooner because he had visibility to the future. Using AI to forecast demand led to better-negotiated prices for the products to maximize revenues and profits at each location.

Goal 3—Finding Insights Not Being Looked For

During the POC, Kent decided to perform correlations to determine how well sales correlated with covers for each meal period. Why? Because it was easy to do with the POC software and could be done on the fly. Kent was doing what humans do when given the time and tools: he was curious and decided to explore that curiosity in the context of the moment.

Figure 10.4 shows the correlation report results where the dinner meal period Sales Dinner is highly and directly correlated (meaning each variable moves in the same direction) to Covers Dinner, as indicated by the three dark gray cell bars or the coefficient of correlation of 0.928 (the value ranges from -1 to +1, with a value of 1 being a perfect correlation). Note that if the user does not know how to interpret the coefficient of correlation, the cell bars provide an intuitive rendition (like a cell phone).

AURORA LightZ Mach 2™	2017 YTD	2016 YTD	YTD Variance	YTD % Variance	Correlation
DINNER					
Sales Dinner	26,243,485	28,184,627	(1,941,142)	(6.89)%	0.928
Covers Dinner	838,256	1,143,641	(305,385)	(26.70)%	1.000

Figure 10.4 Correlation for the dinner meal period.

The high correlation for the meal period was expected, as more sales should be tied to more covers. The "Aha" moment was the unexpected correlation finding for the late night meal period, where Sales Late Night were not correlated (tied) to Covers Late Night. As seen in the correlation report in Figure 10.5, all the cell bars are light gray, with a coefficient of correlation of 0.313 (which is below the typical threshold for two fields being correlated of 0.7).

AURORA *LightZ* Mach 2 ™	2017 YTD	2016 YTD	YTD Variance	YTD % Variance	Correlation
LATE NIGHT					
Sales Late Night	509,495	440,278	69,217	15.72%	0.313
Covers Late Night	15,298	17,603	(2,305)	(13.10)%	1.000

Figure 10.5 Correlation for the late night meal period.

Kent said, "We subsequently learned that waiters were not correctly entering covers in the POS system. This poor data entry led to incorrect data accuracy for cover counts. We remediated the problem by communicating the issue, scheduling training, and monitoring. What we found that we did not specifically ask for was the disconnect at the location and once known, waiters were trained on proper data entry and how to increase customer purchases through menu additions. This training drove up efficiency and revenue and in less than 21 days we cleaned up these bad habits!"

THE ROI OF AI

The POC resulted in a demonstrable value and measurable ROI. From the information, Kent learned how to plan more efficiently, as challenged in Goal 1. AI and analytics revealed that not all discounts were valuable; or, as Kent said, "Discounts are like coupons, only good if it is something that I need," as found in Goal 2. And he learned in Goal 3 that the application of analytics on data revealed things he did not know and did not know to ask for. Table 10.1 reflects a most impressive ROI from the AI-enabled analytics POC *per location*.

Table 10.1 ROI from the analytics POC.

Item – Per Store	Amount
POC analytics implementation cost [one-time & recurring]	($10,750)
Eliminate one Assistant Manager [salary & benefits]	$63,000
Reduce food costs from better AI demand forecast [5%]	$28,000
Reduce beverage costs from better AI demand forecast [5%]	$20,000
Increased profit from liquor volume discounts [top 3 SKUs]	$15,000
Net Annual Benefit Per Store [11× ROI]	**$115,250**

FAILURE IS A CHOICE

Even with the successful POC, the CEO did not have the Mindset for analytics and would not make budget and resources available. Regardless of ROI, the CEO viewed analytics as a cost, and avoiding or reducing cost was more important than an investment to improve restaurant performance. As Kent related, the "CEO believed that if you treat customers right, they will return tomorrow"; he continued that this "is the quintessential example [of the CEO] saying [analytics] is not how we do things."

Without AI-enabled analytics, the restaurant chain incurred no growth and experienced a continued squeeze on profit. Since the COVID-19 outbreak of 2020, the US operations of the restaurant chain have closed, but not necessarily due to Covid: when a new CEO was brought in, he determined that the restaurant was so "broken" that it would be better to close it than to fix the problems. Covid just accelerated the decision!

NOTE

1. Zwerling, R.J. and Sorensen, J.H. (2020). Analytics Roadmap case study. Finance Analytics Institute, LLC, Analytics Academy.

CHAPTER 11

Use Case: Incremental Improvements to Gain Insights

I t may seem counterintuitive, but growth companies are often slow to adopt AI and analytics, especially high-tech industries. Part of this is driven by high margins and part by high growth that masks underlying inefficiencies that cause under-optimized planning. The culture is about meeting demand to grow market share at any cost, since cost is less of an issue when margins are not an issue.

This is the story of Jonathan Morgan, senior director of demand, inventory, and spare parts at Palo Alto Networks (NASDAQ:PANW), a Santa Clara $3.4 billion revenue manufacturer of cybersecurity hardware and software to enable digital transformation across 80,000 customers in 150 countries.[1] Jonathan was at the beginning of the Roadmap to achieve insights from data and was incrementally progressing toward the data-driven Analytics Culture.

Jonathan's scope of responsibilities covered the S&OP process, demand planning, supply planning, inventory management, and spare parts planning.

STARTING ANALYTICS

Jonathan's AI-enabled analytics journey began with reporting data and progressed to the analysis of data for information. In the latter, data visualization and budgeting tools are often used to replace reporting previously done in spreadsheets. From there, desktop statistics and some visualization tools can start providing insights from low-level analytics. Many companies, like PANW, follow this road.

In about 2018, Jonathan was at a conference where he was introduced to analytics, which "got me thinking when we talk about analytics and analysts a lot, and data a lot, and what we do with forecasting . . . we don't truly use analytics the way I [saw] it presented [at the conference]." He evaluated that PANW was really doing reporting, but as the company was growing in volume and complexity, the need for more accuracy in forecasting and optimizing planning would have to be developed beyond the current capabilities.

Jonathan saw that he had to learn more about analytics and advanced analytics to be "predictive and prescriptive" about the business. Further, he and his team had to develop storytelling skills to better inform management, especially if analytics would be part of their presentations. Since executives are less involved with the daily details of the business, the story must be crystalized and simplified.

Johnathan started analytics by hiring a person with a mathematical inclination to do spare parts planning. Although they started with no analytics tools, a report was cobbled together with data and mathematics in Google Sheets to make predictions regarding managing parts at the depots. As depicted in the report in Figure 11.1, spares planning was enhanced in the last column on the right to provide a predictive indication at each depot and part for the Swap Action to take. As Jonathan said, the effort was crude, but they did "get a jump" for better planning.

TEST AND LEARN

Jonathan took a "test and learn" approach to analytics, starting with a small project, measuring the results, and gaining learnings for the next project. In this way, he created a showcase of use cases that could be demonstrated to others for their buy-in.

When Jonathan evaluated his team on the road to analytics, overall, he rated it 2 out of 5 but trending up, as analytics was not yet adopted team-wide. As he looked to expand his team's capabilities in inventory and demand planning, the new people he hired would have a mix of business and analytics backgrounds.

Current inventory and demand models being used did not include "all the right factors, like country requirements, and spreading all the inventory across depots . . . so we need to go deeper into that, and that needs to be driven by analytics, not just to report in Excel or Anaplan. It's gotta (sic) be driven by historical data, as well as different predictive things we can find or indicators we can find, so it helps derive these things and predict and prescribe to us what we need to carry in inventory and what we need to go build."

PANW had the Salesforce CRM system, but a rapidly growing and more complex product portfolio necessitated acquiring new analytics tools and people who could cull through the CRM data to make better decisions about products and customers.

depot	depot_id	part_num	Min	On_Hand	Swap_Qty	serial_num	ourid	rev	qty	flash_aged	sap_aged	Swap_Action
Adelaide ADL-002	ADL	PAN-PA-200-SPR	0	2	2	001606090707	226048	750-000	1	476	476	Excess
Adelaide ADL-002	ADL	PAN-PA-200-SPR	0	2	2	001606090713	226049	750-000	1	476	476	Excess
Adelaide ADL-002	ADL	PAN-PA-7000-100G-NPC-A-FRU	1	1	1	015601002309	261144		1	75	103	Refresh
Auckland B.V. AKL-004	AKL	PAN-PA-200-SPR	4	4	4	001606092558	212263	750-000	1	621	621	Refresh
Auckland B.V. AKL-004	AKL	PAN-PA-200-SPR	4	4	4	001606084210	190165	750-000	1	847	847	Refresh
Auckland B.V. AKL-004	AKL	PAN-PA-200-SPR	4	4	4	001606092695	217394	750-000	1	557	557	Refresh
Auckland B.V. AKL-004	AKL	PAN-PA-200-SPR	4	4	4	001606081198	181191	750-000	1	918	918	Refresh
Albany ALB-004	ALB	PAN-PA-200-SPR	0	1	1	001606090119	241299	750-000	1	297	672	Excess
Amarillo AMA-005	AMA	PAN-PA-200-SPR	0	1	1	001606085114	222637	750-000	1	513	675	Excess
Jordan AMM-002	AMM	PAN-PA-200-SPR	0	1	1	001606081103	223451	750-000	1	476	472	Excess
Amsterdam Def BR B.V. AMS-005	AMS	PAN-PA-200-SPR	15	245	1255	001606050235	157384	750-000	1	934	934	Partial Swap
Amsterdam Def BR B.V. AMS-005	AMS	PAN-PA-200-SPR	15	245	1255	001606049103	135287	N/A	1	1116	1116	Partial Swap
Amsterdam Def BR B.V. AMS-005	AMS	PAN-PA-200-SPR	15	245	1255	001606048091	172402	N/A	1	888	888	Partial Swap

Figure 11.1 Spares planning predictive action report.

Jonathan presented analytics and AI to his executives, who, while generally not seeing analytics as a priority, nonetheless did "not put any brakes" on his efforts. In this case, the executives took a do-no-harm approach to analytics and allowed it to proceed rather than undermining progress. Jonathan indicated that where there were customer-facing activities, senior management had a more proactive view to analytics, like the strategic analytics team in business operations that had an analytics focus—but its "tools are essentially data visualization."

ASSESSING ANALYTICS PERSONAS

Table 11.1 reflects Jonathan's elucidating evaluation of his organization's state of analytics in the context of the tactical Roadmap of Mindset, People, Processes, and Systems. The Personas range from the basic Reporter to the informative Commentator to the Advisor who provides threshold insights. No functional area has the Persona of Strategist who delivers deep insights and foresight, but demand planning is an Advisor trending up to Strategist.

The good news is the recognition of where deficiencies exist in data, skills, or tools so that these can be addressed. When assessing the six functional business areas with respect to the aspirational Persona goals, one is trending down, one is flat, two have been achieved, and two are trending up toward the aspiration.

Moving up the Persona curve will be dependent on acquiring the requisite people and tools. Where data is insufficient, it can easily be remedied once corresponding analytics tools are available. The area of Balance of Inventory Management, while at the lowest Persona of Reporter, was recently recognized as deficient, and thus a program of improvement toward analytical insights would be launched.

In interviewing Jonathan and building the table, he was delighted to walk through this simple benchmark that highlighted where he was compared to where he aspired for his team to be, beyond the Reporter and Commentator. He would present the table to his team to gain consensus and triangulate on requirements and resources for new people and tools to achieve the aspirations. This was an excellent illustration of change management by engaging his team to buy into the

Table 11.1 Roadmap self-assessment by functional area.

Business area	Current Persona and trend	Mindset and People	Reporting	Data	Tools
Demand planning—Sustaining	Advisor	Complete	Complete	Complete	Complete
Demand Planning—NPI	Between Commentator and Advisor Trending down	Lacking supporting Mindset from other parts of PANW, and lacking right people	Lacking the right insight from current reports	Lacking data for analytics	Lacking the right analytics tools
Supply planning	Commentator Trending flat	Inconsistent approach by People, with some looking to be data-driven and others less so	Not many insights, as mostly run by spreadsheets	Lacking data for analytics	Lacking AI-enabled analytics tools
Spare parts planning	Advisor	Complete	Complete	Complete	Complete
Depot inventory management	Commentator Trending up	Getting better with Mindset and hiring People with business and analytics skills	TBD	TBD	Lacking tools for AI-enabled analytics
Balance of inventory management	Reporter Trending up	Have Mindset to Commentator and aspire to Advisor	Spreadsheet reports with plug-in data but don't know if "right" level of inventory is on-hand	Lacking sufficient data	Stuck in Excel

assessment and shape the plan forward. It also emphasized the value of benchmarking to know where you are versus where you want to be and the gap to fill to get there.

As Jonathan gained intelligence about AI and analytics, his focus evolved to educate his team about "how do we optimize and leverage analytics to point us in the right direction and make decisions. . . And that's where the AI stuff and ML will help come into play. I want these tools we have in front of us, and the ones we need to go invest in, helping [us] make decisions or telling [us] what other decisions [we] should be considering."

MOVING FORWARD

Jonathan recounted how the Analytics Academy (by the Finance Analytics Institute) gave him clarity and definition regarding analytics, saying, "I found out I really didn't know what I was talking about [on analytics] or what the potential was or how to describe it. This has helped definitely solidify my understanding of how to approach things and the value you can get out, and articulate that as I speak to people."

Jonathan began his next test-and-learn with another new hire for data analytics. He discovered from his first analytics hire that there are two types of analysts: those who are clever and those who are curious. The first hire was clever in wanting to get hands-on to manipulate data to produce a report. However, their enjoyment came from using tools rather than gaining insights, which meant Jonathan had to be specific about what he wanted the outcome to be (like the report in Figure 11.1).

What is more valuable is the characteristic of being curious about what insights can be obtained from data. Here, Jonathan could be broad and ask the analyst, "How can we optimize inventory?" This is a question without a specific output requirement and leaves a curious person to ask, "What in inventory do you want to optimize, and what benefit or decision are you trying to make?"

This line challenges both parties to think in-depth about the business. It leads the analyst to think more about the scope of data and the application of analytics. The resulting effort will often yield a better outcome than thought when the question was first posed and lead to finding insights that were not initially being looked for.

As Jonathan realized, we tend to gravitate to hire clever people: tool jockeys who enjoy manipulating the tool to deliver a report to answer a highly specific question. Tool jockeys also lack curiosity about what insights may be revealed from the data. The enjoyment comes from manipulating the tool, not the value that can be derived from the data. Jonathan's point was that a curious person seeks to find the insights from data and has a higher value than a tool jockey. Any smart person can be taught a tool, but curiosity is intrinsic to an individual and difficult to teach.

NOTE

1. Zwerling, R.J. and Sorensen, J.H. (2020). Benchmarking & my analytics journey. Finance Analytics Institute, LLC, Analytics Academy.

CHAPTER 12

Use Case: Analytics Are for Everyone

I n some ways, this last case study is the most interesting, as on the surface, it seems the most unlikely environment for analytics.[1] Often we associate the use of AI-enabled analytics with big companies, big data, and herds of data scientists feverishly working on cloud platforms with their machine learning and programming teams to deliver new applications. They boil the ocean with "big data" to do big things. But as we will learn, AI is for all.

The San Antonio Museum of Art (SAMA) is a gem in the museum world, delightfully located on the River Walk in San Antonio, Texas. SAMA is a mid-size 501(c)(3) non-profit organization. In art, beauty is in the eye of the beholder: how can analytics be applied to such a seemingly subjective environment?

This is the story of Lisa Tapp, COO/CFO of SAMA, who received an invitation to attend the Analytics Academy produced by the Finance Analytics Institute. Lisa was attracted by the module "Systems & Storytelling for Data-Driven Decisions" because she wanted to learn how to tell a better story to her Finance Committee. Specifically, she wanted to make her financial packet better and easier to assemble and tell the committee a story that was better understood and informative.

THE ROAD TO ANALYTICS

Although Lisa was not specifically seeking analytics for SAMA, she nonetheless traveled to San Diego, California, to attend two days of courses. She learned how analytics could both solve her primary mission and provide insights that could materially improve business performance.

Lisa's financial packet, like that of most companies, was made from spreadsheets. Because spreadsheets are laborious to prepare, the reporting provided was basic, and she noted the need to "beef up" reports. To elevate reporting, Lisa reached out to other museums and found a few examples that were "beautiful." However, they were built in multiple spreadsheets that had to be manually updated, and the museums took years to develop their reports.

Lisa hoped to find software that could simplify the process. She had tried a database consolidation tool with reporting and dashboard templates that overlaid Microsoft Power BI. However, it was "complicated" to extract the data into a better format for manipulation, and she considered it too difficult to teach to someone else. Further, as she was not a Power BI user, it meant having to learn Power BI and the database tool at the same time.

Accordingly, Lisa needed software that would "stick": that is, it could be learned and used by others so that the reporting and analytics developed did not leave SAMA when she left.

When Lisa was asked why she, in an art world that is creative and seemingly far from the structure of analytics, would be intrigued to attend an Analytics Academy, she responded, "I'm a finance person. And that's why I lean toward this type of thing. . . . I'm naturally analytical." Importantly, she described herself as "curious" and "naturally an out-of-the-box thinker." These last two traits, as we have discussed, are drivers for AI and analytics to be successful.

Most prophetically, Lisa kept this saying on her desk: "No one has ever found a way to improve anything without changing it in some way"—and change is paramount to building the Analytics Culture of data-driven decisions that will improve business performance.

Lisa continued, "It's trying to break a mold, and I think that's what we're doing with Aurora [LightZ™ analytics software] . . . we're breaking a mold in our industry . . . Let's look at [our business] in a different way and see what we find . . . [A]nd I guess that was the scary part . . . you just dig into the data and see what it is going to tell you."

STEPPING INTO ANALYTICS

When SAMA decided to invest in analytics software, Lisa noted that she and her team were stepping into unknown territory: "Certainly, a step of faith, when we did not know where it would take us or what we would see on the other side of our implementation."

Lisa saw analytics as a "Great Adventure." Spending capital on the unknown outweighed the risk of continuing business as usual. The latter would certainly not improve outcomes, whereas the capital risk to engage in analytics was not existential and had the prospect of improving the business. She continued, "If I am not exploring new ways to improve our business, then I am not doing my job."

However, Lisa did not jump into the AI world blindly. She first did a proof-of-concept (POC) test that revealed trends, correlations, and predictions that had never been known and were highly valuable. For example, one correlation revealed that on Saturdays, unemployment was directly correlated with membership sales. This correlation was not specifically being looked for and appeared by simply drilling through the data.

The finding was material because Saturday was the biggest day of the week for membership sales, and the correlation was direct: as unemployment went down, so did membership sales. Apparently, when people have more income security, they spend disposable income in other ways.

To further her point on stepping out, museums have been struggling for some time, and old funding models have not worked as they did in prior years. Moving forward, innovation needs to be part of the culture. However, Lisa was quick to point out that custom vs. innovation was not right or wrong. She saw it as a difference, and joked, "If everybody was like me, we'd be in trouble!" She then added that the process needed to also "allow somebody else's input who is more cautious" and gain a larger perspective to not just see through rose-colored glasses.

Lisa described her analytics journey as a "long road" due not to technical issues but simply to her time availability. Day-to-day life often intrudes on the roll-out of analytics, and that is why we say the journey is not hard, it is disciplined.

Lisa was very pleased with how her team accepted analytics. They now saw data in ways they could not previously, including trends and analysis of trends. Performance measures were often presumed from gut feel and now could be quantified, visualized, and predicted.

Further, SAMA went beyond data visualization to AI. For example, an AI indicator predicted the future of the trend. A spreadsheet can only tell that revenue is down year-over-year. That is easy to feel in the year 2020, as the COVID-19 virus forced the closure of many outlets open to the public. However, what is the future?

A separate report on attendance, shown in Figure 12.1, revealed that year-over-year, Quantity and NetAmount (revenue) were down. But as Lisa noted, the AI-calculated 12 Month Predicted Trend Direction, while signaling the future of the trend to be down at the end of Summer 2020, was rapidly changing in strength as the year progressed.

The arrow shows the future direction of the trend, and the number shows the strength. From September to December 2020, the values of all negative downward arrows were decreasing in negative strength; and by December 2020, NetAmount flipped to a positive upward prediction of the future trend. This AI-predicted trend is very sophisticated and based on a nonlinear equation, but the beauty of this analytics was that Lisa did not have to know mathematics to understand the prediction

AURORA LightZ Mach 2™ PREDICTIONS	12 Months Predicted Trend Direction		12 Months Predicted Trend Direction		12 Months Predicted Trend Direction		12 Months Predicted Trend Direction	
DEMAND	SEP 2020		OCT 2020		NOV 2020		DEC 2020	
Quantity	⬇	(14.09	⬇	(12.78)	⬇	(10.38)	⬇	(7.25)
NetAmount	⬇	(6.41	⬇	(4.78)	⬇	(2.01)	⬆	2.05

Figure 12.1 Trend of prediction.

and gain insight. Having a view to the future contradicted gut feel and supplied the confidence to preclude taking the types of actions related to a declining business versus an improving business outlook.

The other benefit of the analytics platform was how quickly they could navigate through data on the fly to generate reports and charts at a speed that could never be done in spreadsheets. Lisa commented that this alleviated the time-consuming and cascading effort required to make even minor changes in spreadsheets.

Lisa related that there was not a lot of time or bandwidth with a small staff, so with the new software, she had two mints in one. On the one hand, there was a broad range of reporting and charting to satisfy all their operational needs at the touch of a button; and on the other, predictive capabilities were included for the same data.

Further, Lisa commented on the statistical forecasts she obtained and being "completely amazed at how accurate some of those predictions were. [W]hen we were looking at revenue predictions going back and then saying but what did we actually do in October, in November, in December of 2020, with Covid in the whole mix of this, . . . [the] predictions were within $1,000 of our actual [revenue], and I'm like, What! That's like crazy accurate!"

ANALYTICS IS FOR ALL

Lisa started SAMA on an AI and analytics journey that automated and elevated reporting with predictive insights that her team could use to better understand the business and improve performance. She is proof that AI-enabled analytics is not reserved for large companies. On the contrary, any company and any executive who seeks to plan for the future instead of reacting to the future when it arrives can do so with boldness for innovation, a tactical Roadmap to implement AI-enabled analytics, and the discipline to stay on course.

Epilogue

We have methodically walked you through the application of AI and analytics in business and provided the Roadmap to the Analytics Culture for enhanced business performance. While analytics projects have had an abysmal track record, it has been largely due to executives' failure to realize the value of AI and analytics, failure of clarity of vision to a Roadmap to implement analytics, or failure from misalignment/derailment from the Roadmap. These failures are choices that this book has identified and given you the knowledge to correct. As we have repeated, the road to AI-enabled analytics is not long, hard, or expensive—it is simply disciplined!

AI and analytics are not the end of the decision process: they are integral input that combines with human experience and intuition. Analytics provides the highest level of dispassionate and unbiased objectivity. When experience, intuition, and analytics agree, then the objective of the decision has a high probability of occurrence; and when any of these factors are misaligned, it should give pause for deeper thought. Decision-making based on empiricism and analytics is the appropriate balance.

AI is not going away—it is increasing throughout all aspects of life. We are at the dawn of a new century of technology, similar to the tectonic shifts in the twentieth century where society went from the horse and buggy to landing a man on the moon.

In 1900, 41% of the workforce was employed in agriculture. One hundred years later, in the year 2000, that percentage was 1.9%.[1] This dramatic drop was brought about by technology. AI will have a similar impact on today's workforce for both blue-collar and white-collar jobs, and across all industries.

The only jobs AI cannot replace involve human imagination, innovation, curiosity, and leadership. An executive whose primary decision process is motivated about the politics of career will succumb to the executive who embraces AI to unleash their team's curiosity and imagination for the discovery of innovation.

There are four future outcomes for business: those that are the good and will continue to get better, those that are mediocre but will get better, those that are failing and will fail, and those that are good but will decline. No track is permanent, and all can change with leadership. Think Apple, which was once a great company that almost failed but rose to become the highest-valued company in America. The difference was leadership that inspired innovation.

In the year 2021, people are employed to type data into spreadsheets to make reports for management and write ad hoc notes on those reports to explain the results—just as they did in the 1990s. How long is this archaic process going to last, when AI can already make these tasks obsolete? It is time for business to grab hold of AI and analytics and accelerate into the future.

The author Robert J. Ringer notes the following about the Theory of Reality, which advises that "Reality isn't the way you wish things to be, nor the way they appear to be, but the way they actually are. Either you acknowledge reality and use it to your benefit, or it will automatically work against you."[2] AI-enabled analytics is today's and tomorrow's reality: you now have the knowledge and Roadmap to engage it and, with it, command its immense benefits to drive your future business performance.

NOTES

1. Dimitri, C., Effland, A., and Conklin, N. (2005). The 20th century transformation of US agriculture and farm policy. Economic Information Bulletin Number 3. United States Department of Agriculture. https://www.ers.usda.gov/webdocs/publications/44197/13566_eib3_1_.pdf.
2. Goodreads. (n.d.). Robert J. Ringer quote. https://www.goodreads.com/author/quotes/109108.Robert_J_Ringer.

Analytics Champion Framework

The Fundamental Qualifications, Skills, and Project Steps for the Analytics Champion

INTRODUCTION

The Analytics Champion (AC) framework is written for the person assigned the critical responsibility of managing and implementing an AI-enabled analytics pilot and proof of concept (POC) projects and scaling analytics throughout the organization. This framework supplements the Roadmap to implement the culture of data-driven decisions for improved business performance as described in Chapter 5 and provides more specific explanations and discussion in accordance with the implementation steps described in Chapter 7.

Additionally, the framework includes sections on defining analytics champion qualifications, AC skillsets, and starting an analytics project. The framework serves several important purposes: (i) it describes the AC's scope of responsibilities, (ii) it aids in defining the position and within the organization, and (iii) it sets a pathway to sustain analytics and scale it to other organizational departments or functions. This framework has several objectives:

- Describes the requisite qualities and capabilities of an effective AC
- Offers insight for the executive to assign the AC
- Provides important fundamentals to launch AI-enabled projects

The AC and the sponsoring executive are joined at the hip to implement the Analytics Culture and must adhere to the most basic of all ground rules: the executive's unwavering support for the AC; and the AC's candid, complete, and timely communication with the executive. Without this, the Analytics Culture cannot be built and sustained. However, with this mutual assurance, failures, attempted diversions, delays, and resistance to change will be overcome to achieve business performance improvement and career-building successes.

ANALYTICS CHAMPION QUALIFICATIONS

This discussion of the AC's qualifications will help ensure the proper selection of the key individual. This position is tasked to break new ground and, as such, requires an in-depth understanding.

160

Experience and Education

As the AC, the road to analytics must not be your first rodeo; that is, you must not be a stranger to analytics. You must have experience with regression formulas, correlations, Month Carlo simulations, statistics (e.g. standard deviation, coefficient of variation, statistical process control index, etc.), and linear algebra, to name a few.

Further, you must have worked with analytics software (e.g. desktop statistical, data mining, or enterprise AI/analytics platforms or tools). Note that we are not talking about having experience with data visualization tools (e.g. PowerBI, Qlik, Tableau, etc.), which many believe to be analytics tools; we are referring to *real* analytics tools (e.g. R, BigML, Aurora Predictions, etc.) with built-in AI that can assist with finding *real* insights. It is not necessary to be proficient in a tool, but you do need to have some hands-on experience. You do not have to know or have done machine learning (ML) coding or have used Python or R, but you need to know about ML and its process, classifications, divisions, and popular algorithms if your POCs or projects will be using ML.

The AC should have a mathematical background with a Bachelor of Science or equivalent degree in discipline such as economics, finance, math, physics, or engineering.

Project Management Primer

A project is an endeavor undertaken to create a unique product, service, or result. Projects are distinguished from operations in that they have a beginning, a middle, and, most important, an end. All projects should have a defined business outcome/deliverable, an agreed schedule and timeline, and a budget to manage a limited number of people and outside resources (software, consulting, etc.).

All project managers must be skilled in the CTV of a project: Cost, Time, and Value. The Cost is the budget, the Time is the schedule, and the Value is the ROI. Project managers must maintain the CTV or explain and get prior approval for any material deviation. The project manager's success is measured against the CTV.

The AC operating as the project manager can be in a line or matrix organization, whichever is better suited for the company. But the AC must be a project manager as a manager and not as a coordinator, as the latter has no authority over resources.

The AC as the project manager must adhere to the qualifications of sound project management, including Project Manager Key Characteristics, Project Management Key Principles, Project Manager Key Responsibilities, Project Manager Status Reporting, and Project Manager Wrap-up.

Project Manager Key Characteristics

- *Be agile and flexible:* Be adaptive to changing circumstances without loss of bandwidth and focus.
- *Create consistency*: Use standardized processes to achieve consistent delivery.
- *Define roles and responsibilities:* Have a clear understanding of who does what in each phase.
- *Plan projects:* Define the scope and plan the delivery before executing initiatives.
- *Power growth:* Enable the company to grow and scale by using the right processes and capturing the planned information and insights to drive an Analytics Culture of data-driven decisions.

Project Management Key Principles

The AC needs to adhere to six key principles as set forth in Figure A.1. These principles ensure that projects are performed and managed toward the attainment of the project's objectives, stay within planned budget and resources, meet expected timelines, and deliver quality outcomes. Team members also benefit from these principles by being involved in personal enrichment and career enhancement tasks.

Go slow to go fast

Take the time to define the scope and plan the delivery of results before starting execution

Ensure collaboration and alignment

Align project team and business to work toward the same goals

Customer centricity

Put the customer first and continuously solicit their feedback

Iterative delivery

Deliver often and apply customer feedback

Be adaptable

Embrace new ways to maximize value

Time boxed

Instead of working on the task until it's done, you proactively decide how much time you'll spend on it and when

Figure A.1 Project Management Principles for the AC.

Project Manager Key Responsibilities

- ▪ Accountable for all project activities from planning through delivery
- ▪ Manages project *triple constraints* (scope, schedule, budget)
- ▪ Manages project risks and issues, acts as a single point of contact for status, and sponsors executive conflict resolution
- ▪ Ensures that business requirements are met; manages change requests
- ▪ Promotes advocacy of analytics and is proactive in change management practices

The AC is further responsible for developing the project plan in detail; a helpful device is the Gantt chart, a sample of which is depicted in Figure A.2. This graphical visualization informs scheduling, managing, and monitoring specific tasks, resources, milestones, and dependencies in a project. A Gantt chart shows the start and finish dates of tasks and is useful in defining the sequence, interdependencies, and potential bottlenecks of tasks, as well as those that may have been excluded from the project timeline. The Gantt chart aids in communicating project status and plans and helps ensure the project remains on track.

| AI-Enabled Analytics Project | | | | Finance Analytics Institute | | 01-May-21 | 27-May-21 |
| PROJECT NAME | | | | CLIENT NAME | | START DATE | END DATE |

Task ID	Task Name	Start Date	End Date	Duration (in Days)
T01	Problem Definition	5/1/2021	5/2/2021	2
T02	Data	5/3/2021	5/8/2021	6
T03	Analytics Insight	5/9/2021	5/21/2021	13
T04	Insight to Action	5/22/2021	5/25/2021	4
T05	Solution Adoption	5/26/2021	5/27/2021	2

Remarks:
Fast Implementation of Analytics Project

Figure A.2 Sample Gantt chart.

Project Manager Status Reporting

The AC should provide regular project status review sessions with the sponsoring executive and, when appropriate, present to other executives the project highlights of derived benefits from analytics and their impact on data-driven decisions and improved performance. The executive status update should discuss the following key pieces of information:

- *Overall status:* Review the project status since the previous meeting against key dimensions such as budget, schedule, milestones, etc. Often, a project status report summarizes the project's status, as depicted in Figure A.3; the colors are explained in Figure A.4.

- *Scope:* Review accomplishments since the previous meeting: What milestones have been delivered, what feedback has been received, etc.

- *Risk:* Review any risks and discuss the proposed mitigation approach. Highlight risks that have materialized and obtain strategic guidance where necessary.

- *Budget:* Review actuals against planned budget and estimated cost to completion. Propose solutions, if projected to go over budget.

- *Change:* Review any change requests above defined thresholds against scope, cost, and timeline. Maintain a change request log for historical context.

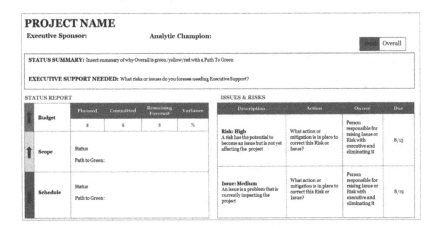

Figure A.3 Project status report

	Green	Yellow	Red
Scope	Scope is stable. No changes which significantly alter the planned high/critical scope. No changes which significantly impact budget, timeline, or effort.	Project is **at risk** of potential changes to the planned high/critical scope; may impact budget, timeline, or effort. And/or: Project lacks alignment on high/critical scope.	Budget, timeline, or effort have been significantly impacted by a change or misalignment on the planned high/critical scope. Escalation and/or change request needed.
Schedule	Major milestone(s) are on track.	Major milestone(s) are **at risk** of being delayed at least 1 or 2 week(s).	Major milestone(s) will be missed by 2 weeks. Escalation and/or change request needed.
Budget	Cost forecast is no more than 5+% for the entire project.	Cost forecast is between 6-10% for the entire project.	Costs for the entire project will exceed forecast by 10+%. Escalation and/or change request needed.

Status trending upward
- **Green**—Does not apply
- **Yellow**—Expected to be green in the next two weeks
- **Red**—Expected to be yellow or green in the next two weeks

Status trending neutral
- **Green**—Expected to stay green
- **Yellow**—Expected to stay yellow by next status report
- **Red**—Expected to stay red by next status report

Status trending downward
- **Green**—Expected to be yellow/red by next status reports
- **Yellow**—Expected to be red by next status report
- **Red**—Expected to continue on a negative path in next status report

Figure A.4 Heat map color explanations.

Project Manager Wrap-up

At the completion of an analytics project, the AC must summarize the results and document the following items:

- Major milestones and deliverables
- Monetized improvements and ROI
- Future improvements in process, people skills, and systems and tools, including data quality issues and accessibility
- Outside resources, e.g. vendors, consultants, etc.
- Future departments to scale the Analytics Culture for data-driven decisions

Analytics Champion Position

When selecting the right AC, an often-misunderstood perception is that the person should be a data scientist. However, while data scientists are statistically strong, they most often lack the requisite business communication, storytelling, and acumen skills.

The AC also should not be from the analyst level in the organization, as they lack experience interfacing with executives, understanding their challenges and needs, and telling the compelling stories that will convince and persuade them to make decisions based on analytics findings. This soft skillset is very rare among analysts and even managers. If analysts had this capacity, then they would probably have been promoted to director level.

On the other hand, the AC should not be too senior, such as at a vice president level. While personalities on this level often have a strong foundation in the soft skillset and might have the hard skills to provide insight for data-driven decisions, not many vice presidents want to move from a job where they are leading larger organizations to a project manager role as an AC with a few (or just dotted line) reports.

As such, the AC should be found among mid-level managers who have a deep understanding of analytics techniques and tools gained from prior positions and may have had a job as a director of finance, operations, marketing, etc. where they focused on providing insights using both soft and hard skillsets.

The mid-level manager who takes the AC role has advanced the analytics agenda in businesses and will see the AC position having direct access to executives and networking across the entire organization. With this exposure and a successful job as an AC, the person can be a perfect candidate for a higher-level position down the road.

Soft Skills

As we have seen throughout the book, the AC operates with a wide range of hard skills, understanding the techniques to generate insight to influence decisions and foresight to impact the strategic direction. The AC must also be a master of soft skills, including *communication, collaboration, business acumen,* and the ability to lead at the *strategic leadership* level.

Communication

Communication is often underestimated. Good communicators (i) know their audience and speak directly to them and not at them, (ii) have a customized approach to each executive, (iii) understand that what resonates with one executive might not resonate with another, and (iv) know how to deliver a *relevant* message that is not generic and is *focused*, as time is a valued asset for executives.

Making a meaningful connection to executives means telling a *compelling* story that entices them to learn more. In the process of telling these stories, visuals are often an effective way of expressing data, as a chart often tells more than raw numbers in a table. It is frequently forgotten that presenting to executives is often not a monologue but a dialogue, where further clarification and new ideas become a part of the conversation. Therefore, the AC should communicate clearly and concisely (written and verbal), be familiar with business terminologies, adjust the language to meet the executive's needs, and anticipate potential questions.

Finally, and most important when communicating with insights gained from advanced analytics, simplify complexity: since the tools and techniques to generate the analytics findings are complex, they should not be part of the communication. Include the facts, what the facts mean at a high level, and then the conclusion and suggested actions.

Collaboration

Collaboration is a working practice where individuals join forces for a common purpose to achieve business benefit and considers the ideas, skills, experiences, and opinions around the organization. When individuals work together openly, goals become more aligned, which is the foundation of a higher success rate.

Collaboration with the business provides a better understanding of business operations as well as knowledge about how changes in one part of the business might affect another. Several factors are important for effective collaboration: *trust, tolerance, debate, and self-awareness.*

Collaboration is based on building relationships, and at the foundation of every relationship is *trust.* If you don't trust people, then you are constantly validating what they are doing or what they have been presenting. This wastes time and can invalidate a project. Trust comes from having experienced work products from others and knowing that their work was both timely and competent. Ensure that trust exists, or take the requisite action to realign the people in the project to get it.

In the workspace, we often meet people from different backgrounds or cultures, but people can also be biased. As such, their values, perspectives, and opinions may deviate from those of the

AC. Therefore, the AC will not be able to appreciate or value input from others without a fair amount of *tolerance*. Listen to people with different backgrounds, cultures, or opinions with open ears, as respecting other's opinions is needed to ensure the open and candid *debate* that is necessary to achieve the project's Cost, Time, and Value.

Self-awareness plays a significant role in effective collaboration, as your emotions, motivations, and blind spots can have a significant effect on people around you. Self-awareness is often developed using feedback from others, as well as external techniques or tools. Without self-awareness, the AC may move in a direction that might be personally relevant but not relevant for the sponsoring executive or company.

ACs performing at the highest levels are the glue in organizations and are never left out of a decision process because they are capable of applying analytics that generates insight for data-driven decisions.

Business Acumen

Business acumen can be distilled down to understanding how a company makes money. It is often seen as the ability to be business savvy or the talent of having business sense. It has its roots in keenness and quickness in understanding and dealing with business situations with the purpose of leading to a positive outcome.

Business acumen for the AC is to first understand the organization's operating model. This includes an understanding of the key performance indicators (KPIs) and strategic objectives (discussed in Chapter 8), as well as deep knowledge about the mechanisms and complexities that define the business.

Taking business acumen to the next level adds a deep understanding of how one area of a company affects or impacts other areas. Understanding these relationships is crucial when optimizing the entire company's performance. The most advanced level of acumen is understanding how a change in the competitive landscape affects the company or line of business.

Strong business acumen can be obtained through many sources. Finding a business leader who can explain the strategy and becoming comfortable with the company's financials is essential in the process of building acumen. Reading the business intranet can be a solid source to gain business understanding. Many internal and external sources can also be helpful, such as listening to the company's and competitors' quarterly earnings calls, paying attention to business news for the industry, and listening to customers' feedback.

Strategic Leadership

Some people are born leaders, but most leadership is acquired through education, experience, and self-confidence achieved by experiencing failure and success. While some people are more naturally suited to leading others, everyone moving into a leading position needs to develop a skillset for leadership.

Probably the most common mistake among leaders is not knowing the difference between managing and leading. *Managing* relates to job competency and being able to perform a task, whereas *leading* relates to the ability to inspire, influence, and elevate people. As such, the ability to lead has characteristics including being able to encourage others to do new things, being able to influence others to make new decisions, and inspiring others to go above and beyond.

Strategic leadership means having a strategic vision for a group and motivating and persuading others to acquire that vision. Strategic leadership has four components, as shown in Figure A.5: *strategic thinking, strategic acting, strategic influencing, and strategic thought leader*[1]:

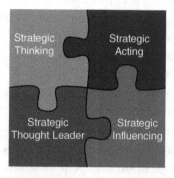

Figure A.5 Components of strategic leadership.

Strategic thinking is the understanding of complexity, ambiguity, and the interplay between the business and its internal and external environment. Grasping the bigger picture and having detailed knowledge of the business operation will enable an understanding of how the business generates revenue, profit, and cash flow. Especially in larger corporations, it is necessary to know how changes in lines of business affect each other and have a deep understanding of the market/competitive landscape, as well as how changes in external economic factors influence performance. This knowledge is the foundation for strategic thinking to recognize the options, risks, and opportunities available for problem-solving and future business performance.

Strategic acting is the ability to take decisive action consistent with the strategic direction for the business. The vision and mindset of the AC need to align with the business strategy. The mindset is aligned with both the short- and long-term strategic intent of the business. It is essential to learn constantly from the efforts or attempts made in the execution of the business strategy. This is a continuous process to always act in alignment with the business strategy and keep the analytics findings relevant in relation to it.

Strategic influencing is the ability to convincing other departments to adopt the suggestions of your department. It is about the willingness to stick your neck out, take measured risks, and get out of your comfort zone to influence an executive's business decisions. The AC uses their analytics toolbox to identify problems, risks, and opportunities to generate business insight and foresight. With their persuasive communication skills, the AC can challenge, influence, and convince the executives to committed actions.

A *strategic thought leader* has the ability to consistently answer the biggest questions from business executives by having the right alignment of people, processes, and systems. The AC understands how to utilize modern tools and techniques and builds a strong support team with the right talent, experience, and passion to always execute despite the complexity of an executive's requests.

Character

The AC must be prepared to face many challenges when pursuing AI-enabled analytics, whether during the initial departmental pilot or as analytics is scaled to subsequent departments. These challenges may involve the pilot department posing barriers to the project by withholding data, failing to highlight risks and operating changes, and/or limiting the bandwidth of previously assigned resources (discussed in Chapter 6). When these issues occur, it is reassuring to remember what General Norman Schwarzkopf said: "Leadership is a potent combination of strategy and character. But if you must be without one, be without the strategy."[2] The AC must have two key characteristics: *resilience to resistance* and *always an option to be found*.

Resilience to resistance. The AC likely will need to confront and overcome various methods of resistance. It is necessary to garner the support of your sponsoring executive and develop a plan to manage resistance and incorporate techniques to *build a sense of urgency, select the right team,* and *build on success*:

> *Build a sense of urgency:* Set the tone for why analytics is important to do. Research has demonstrated that "people change what they do less because they are given analysis that shifts their *thinking* than because they are shown a truth that influences their *feelings*."[3] Figure A.6 summarizes an approach that might benefit you within your organization.

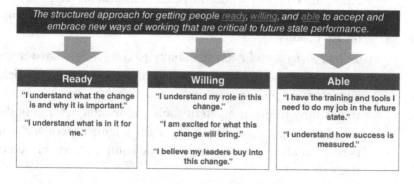

Figure A.6 Ready, willing, and able.

Ways to communicate a sense of urgency include calculating the monetary benefit resulting from the project (e.g. if we make this improvement to our sales forecast, we can reduce the cost of carrying inventories by 10% or $10 million). Money "talks" and often creates a path to expediency.

Select the right team: Doing this ensures that your project will be able to deflect or minimize the usual nay-sayers. Team members who have earned the respect of peers, have demonstrated skills and capabilities, and are recognized as effective communicators will shine a spotlight on the project's potential and encourage others to remain open-minded about the project's outcomes.

Build on successes: Building on success earns more support to continue to build more success, which will provide reputation, resources, and momentum to the overall project. This creates the opportunity to determine what to tackle next, then create another project, and so on until the Analytics Culture becomes embedded in the organization.

Always an option to be found. The AC faces surprises and unanticipated impediments to successfully performing and completing the pilot project. These challenges include *known unknowns* and *unknown unknowns.* The AC should anticipate impediments, but their precise nature does not reveal itself until they occur.

When this happens, the course of action is to seek alternatives to what was initially planned. For example, if the project is capturing historical data, but numerous errors are discovered, then the pilot might find an alternative data source or limit the volume of data so that it can be corrected and made useful. Another example might be the reassignment of a promised team member. If this occurs, the AC might explore finding talent in another department that can be loaned to the pilot project.

These and other examples are challenges that the AC can overcome with persistence and support from the sponsoring executive, to stay focused on the ultimate benefits to be derived from the project.

Know the Ground Rules

The AC must know and set the *ground rules* with the sponsoring executive and analytics team to ensure setting realistic expectations, sustaining executive support, managing project scope, and having a structured and pragmatic project. The sponsoring executive and AC must firmly establish and agree to the ground rules and take the attitude that they are in the foxhole together and will only prevail through mutual support and adherence to those ground rules. The rules include *setting realistic expectations, sustained executive support, managing project scope,* and *being structured and pragmatic.*

Setting realistic expectations includes four keys to setting clear expectations:

Realistic goals: Set expectations that inspire and challenge people to stretch themselves but are realistic and don't strain people. If you overstretch people, they will burn out, and you will undermine their motivation, performance, and well-being.

Clearly articulated goals: Goals are best when written as it forces clarity of thought and necessitates explaining with confidence and clarity to team members and other stakeholders *why* the expectations are essential to the overall goals and strategy.

Discuss and gain agreement to the expectations: This ensures gaining the team's commitment and support for effective implementation. However, be sure this is a consultation process and not a democratic process, as the AC retains the ultimate prerogative to decide on the final set of expectations that will be applied.

Communicate expectations continuously: Continuous communication reinforces intentions and expectations. These should be communicated at every opportunity, including team meetings and events, coaching conversations, etc.

Sustained executive support is essential for the success of a project and is directly related to the strength and visibility that the sponsoring executive demonstrates to the AC. Note, too, that the success of the project requires the AC to maintain candid and continuous communications with the sponsoring executive throughout the project.

Managing project scope requires both ensuring that the tasks to complete are completed and, as necessary, avoiding *scope creep*, which can undermine a project. Scope creep is insidious and causes projects to run longer. As a result, a project consumes more resources, delays the realization of benefits, and becomes more complex, thus disheartening the project team and jeopardizing executive support by undermining credibility that the project is on track to solve the defined problem and achieve the planed ROI and operating benefits.

Being structured and pragmatic. This is the AC's pathway to success: it requires the initial plan to be developed with a clear structure and a pragmatic approach that enables the team to understand each task and recognize why it is important to follow the plan as closely as possible. However, almost without exception, events occur that necessitate refinements to the plan. When that happens, it is incumbent that the project manager is adaptable, makes appropriate adjustments to the work plan, and ensures that the implications of these adaptations are timely communicated to affected project participants and sponsors. The AC must be pragmatic and is at the forefront in setting realistic milestones, timelines, achievable outcomes, and measurable ROI.

ANALYTICS CHAMPION SKILLSETS

The AC needs certain skills and perceptions that are often not taught or experienced, and the AC must also identify those in the implementation team. These include *Systematic Thinking™, Data Definition, Skills Supporting Analytics,* and *Storytelling*. These items provide the foundation for approaching, processing, collaborating, and communicating throughout the POC and analytics scaling projects. What follows was developed by the Finance Analytics Institute as taught at FAI's Analytics Academy.

Systematic Thinking™

All projects start with a problem, goal, or deliverable; but as my grandpa used to say, "The hardest part of a project is to start it." So, where to start an analytics POC? As will be discussed in the next section, the place to begin is with something of material value. OK, what makes value material? Apparently we are on a path of digging a seemingly endless hole of questions. So, to quote my grandpa again, "When you find that you're digging yourself into a hole . . . stop digging." Here is where we engage *Systematic Thinking*, which is

---

A methodology to analyze data by assembling it in a logical hierarchy and applying unbiased analytics to yield insights

---

It is a disciplined engineering approach to identify and solve problems, goals, or deliverables. There are five components of Systematic Thinking:

- *Question:* About the problem/goal
- *Hypothesis:* What the answer is to the question
- *Data:* To answer the question
- *Mathematics:* To apply the data to gain insights
- *Dimensions:* The segments to organize the data into a logical hierarchy

The most important component is developing the Question, as a right answer will follow a right question. As any researcher will tell you, the answer is comparatively easy to attain once the right question is found. From the Question, we can proceed methodically to an answer through a structured hierarchy of applying mathematics on data. For example, problems can be approached through the figurative representation of a plant through its systems, equipment, and parts, as shown in Figure A.7.

Any plant (manufacturing, power generation, recycling, etc.) can be organized into a hierarchy of systems, and within each system a collection of equipment, which itself is composed of parts. This is the logical hierarchy in which data will be arranged, to which analytics are applied to yield a solution to the problem. Consider the Question "How can plant reliability be increased?" An answer is via data analytics, to find the critical path where single or multiple failures in specific parts could shut down the plant.

A plant can be most any representation. For example, a car is composed of systems: say, the engine cooling system, which is composed

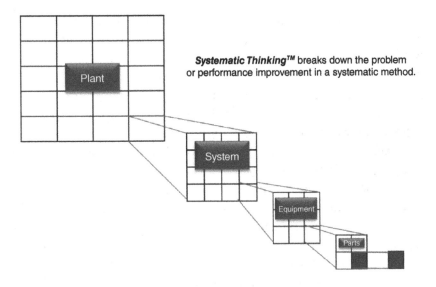

Figure A.7 Systematic thinking about a plant.

of equipment like the water pump and radiator, as well as parts that compose the water pump (impeller, casing, gaskets, etc.). The purpose of this example was to think systematically and hierarchically. Now let us look at a business exercise, this time in healthcare.

A healthcare insurance company deals in risk; that is, an insurance policy's price should be tied to the claims predicted to be paid. A man 35 years old should have a lower premium than a man 85 years old because of the smaller anticipated claims for health services. However, if the younger man has an unanticipated heart attack, the resulting healthcare costs would be significantly more than the premium. If the insurance company received too many of these unanticipated claims, it could face financial collapse. While an insurance company wants to sell more policies, it wants to sell the *right* type of policies: those with lower risk.

Recall the example in Chapter 7 of a major health insurance company. It began a POC by asking how to improve profits but recognized that *profits* by itself was an overly broad term encompassing the entire business. The process to crystallize the problem is the Question component in Systematic Thinking.

In this case, the problem must be large enough to have material benefit yet small enough for a POC. The area of a Small Group (SG) was chosen as it balanced size and materiality. An SG is defined as employers that have from 2 to 50 employees. The Question that was developed regarded profitability vs. size of the group, which revealed that a group with two employees could be profitable as long as the group was healthy (i.e. making fewer claims). Health was more important than size when driving profitability, but a bigger healthy group also generates a higher volume of profit.

After several more iterations, the problem developed into the size of the group, the health of the group, and whether the group would churn (i.e. not renew its contract), and knowing whether churn would happen with six months advance notice (so the insurance company would have time to take action to retain the customer). As such, the POC problem—or Systematic Thinking Question—became, "Which larger size Small Group customers with 25 to 50 employees, in the top two quartiles of health ratings, have a propensity to churn in the next six months?"

With the Question established, Systematic Thinking proceeds to the components of Hypothesis, Data, Mathematics, and Dimensions. The Hypothesis purported that some internal data existed to which the application of mathematics could predict churn. Table A.1 arranges the remaining components of Data, Dimensions, and Mathematics to answer the Question based on the Hypothesis.

The Question has been established about the Small Group, so this is the "plant" as an analogy to Figure A.7. Large is the "system," Healthy is the "equipment," and Input Data is the "part." Note, too, that this is a hierarchical organization of the Dimensions to apply math to the data.

Several elements were chosen for the data, along with the application of mathematics. The first was that customer satisfaction would be a driver of renewal. The hypothesis is that a satisfied customer should be correlated as less likely to churn. However, calculating the R-squared coefficient of correlation required a time series of customer satisfaction data that was not available. As such, this path of exploration was not viable.

Table A.1 Definition of Hypothesis, Data, Math, and Dimensions.

SG	Large	Healthy	Field of Cancel	Math	Note
Dimension	Performance Dimension	Dimension	Input Data	Calculated Data	
SG Customers	>25 members	Blue	Customer Satisfaction	Threshold	Point in time
		Green	Competitive Price	Threshold	What threshold
			Network	Inferential	Personal vs. Group
			Broker Incentive	Threshold	What threshold
			PIC	Velocity	Bingo !

The next data element was to determine whether the price of the policy was correlated with the customer, because if a company can get a policy for materially less, that customer may be more likely to churn. The problem with this data was finding a threshold that could work across policies. An employer often has multiple policies that it offers its employees: what are the product portfolio mix and pricing that become non-competitive? This also feeds into the Network data element: the healthcare providers associated with the policy. The network is subjective to the employee, and this subjectivity had no associated data. As such, too many variables and the lack of key data eliminated both data elements from further consideration.

Broker Incentive was evaluated to find a correlation between what different insurance companies were paying in commission to brokers for each policy. Since the insurance company sold its policies through independent brokers, the hypothesis was that incentive drives behavior, and brokers would move their customers to where the broker made the most commission. However, the attempt yielded no correlations that were materially reliable to predict churn.

Finally, the insurance company explored positive in-group change (PIC), where employees upgrade their policies (e.g. an employee switches from an HMO to a PPO). The Hypothesis was that the employer would allow PICs if it planned to continue with the current insurance company but would not permit PICs if a change to a new insurance carrier was in the works (as changes typically are planned months in advance).

A first derivative was applied to PIC data to calculate a *velocity* of the PIC and whether that velocity was positive or negative. A back-test on this approach confirmed statistically significant reliability to predict whether a customer would churn six months in advance.

Note that while several solution options were considered, each was quickly dispositioned and the solution identified.

Data Definition

The AC must be cognizant of certain data terms to deal with when approaching AI and analytics. First are big data and real-time data, but what makes data *big* in size and *real* in time? Further, ML needs high-quality data to train the model, but what makes data *high-quality*, and what if the analytics is not using ML? These questions often stop analytics projects before they start. Users will capitulate by assuming they do not have big, real, or high-quality data and therefore must have an IT data-cleaning project before attempting analytics—or, worse, that the data simply is not and will not ever be sufficient. This can be true, but only for a small minority of instances. In general, what is needed is *right-size* data, *right-time* data, and *sufficient-quality* data:

> **Right-size data** is data needed by the analytics for the problem identified to be solved, whereas *big data* is hard to define. According to the *Definitions from Oxford Languages from Google*, the definition of *big data* is "extremely large data sets that may be analyzed computationally to reveal patterns, trends, and associations, especially relating to human behavior and interactions." And here's another definition from a Google search: "Big data refers to the large, diverse sets of information that grow at ever-increasing rates." It seems the definition of *big data* evades quantification, as well it should since the volume of data we can consume changes over time. As such, *big data* is a misnomer.
>
> In the 1980s, 10 MB was thought big. By the 2000s, 100 GB was thought big. In 2020, you can buy a 256 GB thumb drive for

$30. Therefore, is big data for analytics 10 MB, 10 GB, 10 TB, or larger? The answer is that the size you need depends on what you are solving, predicting, or optimizing.

For example, a global multi-billion-dollar technology company was interested in applying analytics on its annual recurring revenue contracts across all products and customers in all regions. This required raw data contained in a 350 MB file consisting of 72 million data cells with three years of history. Is this big data? It does not matter, as it is the right size of data for the analytics to be applied.

Right-time data depends on what is being studied. Whereas, is real-time data by the day? Hour? Minute? Second? Tenth of a second? Trillionth of a second?

If your business is setting the world's atomic clock, you are working in 10^{-9} seconds per day. However, to do the S&OP for a typical manufacturing company, you are working on a weekly or monthly basis.

As such, we can turn our heads away from IT speak about *real-time data* and instead focus on reality, which is about *right-time data*, where *right* depends on what we are doing with the data *and* when the data is available. The latter is the most defining property. For example, if we need accurate financial data, it is often unavailable until after the end of the month when the financials are tied out and the month is closed. Therefore, right-time financial data is monthly.

IT can go off in absurd directions because they are not bounded by the practicalities of business. For example, a friend was excited to show me a real-time forecasting application he developed. Taking data synchronously from a telecom switch by the second, the level of traffic was displayed on the screen and updated second by second. Then he said, "Watch this!" as he clicked a button to display the trend for the last 10 seconds plus a forecast for the next 20 seconds.

But wait, there's more: he said, "The forecast uses a linear regression formula. Now watch as I change the forecast formula to a polynomial." My friend was gushing with pride as a simple mouse click was all it took to change the formula. He turned to me and asked, "What do you think?" I responded, "What's the accuracy of the forecast?"

My friend had a puzzled look on his face and replied, "What do you mean, accuracy?" I explained that when a forecast is made, it needs to be back-tested to determine the level of accuracy to predict the actual network traffic, and—here's the punch line—that the forecast only has utility if it is accurate within a band of planning tolerance.

With another puzzled look, he said, "What do you mean, accurate? I can't tell if it's accurate!" With frustration in his voice, he reminded me that I just saw a real-time forecast from real-time data and flipped between different forecast formulas with one click. What more did I want or need?! For him, forecasting for the sake of forecasting in real time was the victory, and the accuracy of the forecast was irrelevant.

"OK," I said, "but what makes this real time? I mean, isn't there a lot of noise if you're measuring in seconds? Would minutes be a better time series and still be real time?" These questions were becoming annoying, as I had not yet given an accolade to his work. His response was, "Why work in minutes when seconds are available?"

I gave it one more try and asked, "Who would use this application, and how would the forecasting be applied?" Exasperated at this point, he simply said that everyone wants real-time forecasting and nothing more needs to be discussed.

For my dear and respected colleague, real time was measured in seconds, regardless of the application. This is a complete disconnect with reality, but for him, at least, it is a definition. As a thought exercise, let us accept the notion that real-time data is data measured in the time interval of seconds. Does this mean if data is not available by the second, it is inadequate or irrelevant? Well, no!

It is about right-time and not real-time data, which depends on the application of what we study and the availability of the data. For most applications across finance, manufacturing, marketing, supply-chain, HR, sales, and so on, data by the second is both unnecessary and unavailable. As such, although our data may not be real-time in the eyes of my colleague, this is both irrelevant and a misnomer. Data needs to be right-time.

Sufficient data quality has been a subject of inquiry across the many lectures we have given to many hundreds of people in many dozens of industries. Fortunately, most people consider their data quality acceptable for analysis; however, a large minority believe their data is insufficient or inadequate to use in analytics. We hear common phrases like "My data is not clean," "We don't have enough data," or "We don't have enough high-quality data." Yet in our expansive experiences, there have been extremely few instances where there was insufficient data.

The problems with data are mostly related to perception, not reality. People think they have inadequate data because they have been told by IT that the data is dirty, or they have heard of an ML project that has failed or stalled due to bad data, or they simply have no confidence in their data. The latter results from working with the data and experiencing issues where a customer name is wrong or an address is missing; after several of these errors, people believe the data has little value for analytics.

As we have discussed with right-size data and right-time data, there is also a similarity between sufficient data quality and high-quality data. Sufficiency is gauged by what we are trying to study with the data. Also, the sufficiency of data quality depends on the techniques being applied to the data.

Financial, inventory, sales, supply-chain, and most support function data is relatively "good": 95% accurate or better. Sure, there are errors interspersed, but they're exceptions. We may harp on the errors because they breed added work and exasperation, both of which skew our perception of the quality of the data.

The next step to determine the sufficiency of data is the technique to be applied to the data. For example, if the technique is arithmetic, then the numbers being added need only be accurate. Further, we may tolerate rounding numbers or a few numbers being wrong because it does not materially affect the outcome.

However, for most ML algorithms, *sufficient* data quality must be *high-quality*. For example, suppose an ML program is being trained to recognize a dog. Thousands of images of dogs—and only dogs, of different varieties—must be input for the algorithm to recognize a dog not included in the training data. If 10,000 images of a variety of dogs are input and there are 100 cats or a preponderance of German Shepherds, then the ML will not be adequately trained and will fail too many times to recognize an image of a dog.

The data accuracy for simple addition of the inventory count in a warehouse with hundreds of thousands of units will be different than the accuracy for data to study multi-variable correlations of life-threatening effects from drug interactions. Therefore, *sufficient* is accurate to the level needed for what is to be studied and the application of the technique to be applied to study the data.

Since we most do not often work on life-or-death outcomes but rather on business performance improvement, we access sufficient quality data throughout our ERP, CRM, POS, inventory, data warehouse, data marts, and (spreadsheets that pull the data from these sources).

Skills Supporting Analytics

As the AC, you need to have and surround yourself with people with the essential capabilities of being *curious, smart,* and *business savvy.* The discussion that follows defines these capabilities and contrasts them, respectively, against being *clever, average,* and *IT savvy.* As we shall see, these are distinctions with differences:

Curious vs. clever: As the AC, you are required to be curious about data, and you need the people who work on the POCs and projects to be curious as well. As we have discussed, there is *curious* and there is *clever.*

When staff are asked for a report, listen to their answer to measure whether they are clever or curious. A clever employee will answer, "I can get that done in a minute." But a curious employee will respond, "What decision are you trying to make?" The former is thinking about how to get the tool to deliver the data, while the latter understands the insights needed to make a better informed decision.

For the clever, it is about using a tool: the focus is on technology first, and the business problem or optimization being sought is secondary. Excel jockeys tend to be clever and most often not curious, as their enjoyment comes from using the tool to get a specified report rather than exploring data for insights that may drive better business performance. Clever people also spend their time making elegant and colorful dashboards; whether these are relevant to making better decisions is beside the point.

A clever person thinks more in IT terms about reporting data. For example, the director of finance of an online B2C company saw a demonstration of the application of AI and analytics. He asked which regression formula the AI applied to forecast, saying that "without a special formula, there was no competitive advantage." He failed to understand that the value to the business was *accurate long-range* forecasts. A special formula may be clever, but if it is not accurate, it is rubbish. As such, if you are surrounded by clever people, the prospect of delivering insights is in peril.

Smart vs. average: Most people are average at what they do. Being average is not a pejorative here; it is simply the definition of any group, be it data or people, having an average. However, when doing analytics POCs and projects, average will not do, as you will be embarking on new ground in tools, techniques, technology, and culture. Therefore, you and your team need to be above average to break ground and lead others into the "promised land."

Smart is more than raw IQ; it dovetails back to *curious*, an inherent nature to question and want to learn, and the ability to learn quickly. Smart people adapt when confronted with a situation they have not experienced. They observe, quickly assimilate the input, and then interact with their environment to continue learning and improving on the adaptation.

An essential characteristic of smart folk is perseverance: not that average people don't have this trait, but it tends to be more prevalent and stronger with the smart. This trait is essential to be able to plow through the many failed experiments that eventually produce success.

People who are smart and curious can be taught a tool and become proficient in that tool, but a clever person who is proficient in a tool often cannot be taught to be curious. Excel and dashboard jockeys are brilliant artisans with their tools, but they are not often able to make the leap to new tools and technologies and thus will not be the vanguards to a culture of AI-enabled analytics for data-driven decisions.

Business savvy vs. IT savvy: As we have written extensively, analytics is for the business user and must be driven by the business user. As such, the successful AC comes from the business, not IT, and is in a mid-management position to ensure a level of business communication and collaboration skills.

A person from IT should not be the AC, because although they may have a good collaboration and communication skills in IT, their interactions with the business have typically been limited. While IT folk can have credibility with their vendors and peers, the IT director will rarely be viewed as a peer by the business.

This is not to say that the IT-savvy person is not respected or liked by the business. It merely points to the fact that they lack the experience to know in detail how the business works since those intricacies can only come from years of experience in the business.

Storytelling

Mark Twain said, "I didn't have time to write a short letter, so I wrote a long one instead."[4] Good storytelling needs to take Mr. Twain's humor on brevity to heart, as well as the traits of clarity and a compelling call to action. For example, take this strategic statement from Southwest Airlines: "Meet customers' short-haul travel needs at fares comparable with the cost of automobile travel." This is how it appeared in a *Harvard Business Review* article in May 2001.[5] Now, fast-forward 20 years to the Southwest mission statement on its website (https://mission-statement.com/southwest-airlines): "Dedication to the highest quality of Customer Service delivered with a sense of warmth, friendliness, individual pride, and Company Spirit."

Both statements are brief, but the second lacks clarity and is not compelling. With the former statement, every employee of Southwest is self-actualized to what their company does and how they are to do it. Southwest is a short-haul carrier, not international. The fares are to compete with the cost to travel by car; no first-class here. The statement smacks of bare-bones with no frills. Just get the customer from point A to point B at a low fare. The customer is also on-board with this statement, as anyone who has flown on Southwest knows not to expect comfort, just a short-haul low price.

However, the latter statement is ambiguous. What business is the company in? The feel-good business? Who is more important, the customer or the individual pride of the employee? What does "Company Spirit" mean? What should my expectations be as a customer? Super-duper customer service? First class? The answers to these questions are uncertain.

As such, brevity must also strive for utility, which will dovetail to storytelling with analytics for management because brevity with utility is required. Figure A.8 shows the path of typical Hollywood stories. Notice that none follow a straight line, but all end at the same point: a happy ending.

If we take the path of the top line, our hero will start his day with sunshine and meet the girl of his dreams, followed by love blossoming. Then things take a turn for the worse, and the happy couple breaks apart. However, love prevails, and they get together to live happily ever after. While this path may be good for movies, it will go down in flames in a presentation to management. What is needed in business is a story that follows a straight line.

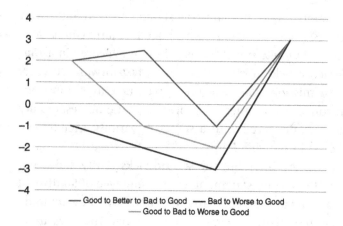

Figure A.8 Path of Hollywood stories.

A good business story for management has four parts:

- Clear and concise *problem summary*
- *Analysis* that identifies the *facts*
- *Evaluation* of what the *facts mean*
- *Conclusion* and *recommendation*

The summary should be about 1–3 minutes, the rest is done within 10–20 minutes, and it is all contained in 10 to 20 lightly filled slides, half of which have visualizations. First, let us see an example of a "bad" story of a presentation by a consultant to the CEO of a chain of grocery stores that had in-store bakeries.

The chain was experiencing rapid growth, but the CFO was concerned that growth was masking underlying defects in the business and asked the consultant for analysis on the data to learn about the operation of the bakeries. The consultant reported back in a meeting to the CFO and CEO:

> I've got bad news: you're losing 15 cents on every sale in your in-store bakeries.
>
> The analytics are clear that price is not correlated with sales.
>
> Further, the velocity of sales is negative, indicating that future sales trends will decline.
>
> You need to raise prices or cut costs or both before the efficiency of the trend line of sales crosses beneath the trend line of expenses.

While the story was brief and to the point, the CEO did not believe the consultant and showed him the door. Fast-forward the clock, and as growth slowed, the bakeries did indeed start hemorrhaging money, because they were losing 15 cents on every sale as reported by the consultant. But by then it was too late to take corrective action other than to close the bakeries.

This story was "bad" because it (i) dropped the conclusion at the beginning without any orientation, (ii) talked in analytical terms the CEO didn't know, (iii) did not first prove there was a problem the CEO agreed with, and (iv) offered solutions that were too broad and not targeted: i.e. was the problem with one SKU or all of them? And was the problem in one store or many?

Let's redo the story, following the rules of concise summary, analysis, evaluation, conclusion, and recommendation:

> Mr. CEO, we've done a detailed analysis of sales and costs in conjunction with the CFO at each in-store bakery in our chain.
>
> The good news is that YoY sales have grown in double digits, but we've grown so fast that we haven't put an eye on cost.
>
> The consolidated revenue and cost year-to-date show a loss of $1 million, equating to an average of 15 cents per unit sold.
>
> The bad news is that the forecast for the next 12 months by store managers and an unbiased statistical forecast both predict sales will be down 17%.
>
> Recommend we immediately (i) close the 12 smallest in-store bakeries, (ii) increases prices on all cakes by 4%, and (iii) centralize ingredient purchasing for all stores, targeting to reduce costs 7%.

This is a "good" story because it (i) sets the stage for what was done and gives it credibility by being detailed and with an accurate source of data, (ii) sets up the problem that costs are out of sync with high-growth sales, (iii) consolidates the problem into something digestible, (iv) confirms the forecasts two ways, and (v) gives specific recommendations for what needs to be done, where, and when. The story is *clear, concise, credible, and compelling.* Notice that although analytics was used, there was no discussion of analytics. But why?

In the movie *A Few Good Men*, the base commander played by Jack Nicholson tells the defense attorney played by Tom Cruise, "You can't handle the truth!" For the commander, smart men and superior officers were incapable of understanding why the soldiers who man the wall must sometimes do things that appear reprehensible to those who bask in the comfort of their efforts. Setting aside the morality of the movie, the analogy is poetic to executives who "can't handle the analytics!" That is, most will not be able to comprehend the application of such things as nonlinear algebra, exponential smoothing, or derivative equations and thus dismiss what they cannot understand.

Storytelling for management is the straight path in Figure A.9 with a beginning, middle, and end. Begin with the summary and then, as in the 1950s TV cop series *Dragnet*, present "just the facts" for the analysis. The middle is an evaluation of what those facts mean, and the end is the conclusion from the evaluation and the recommendation for the solution. That's it!

Figure A.9   Story path for management.

To deliver a concise and compelling story for management, here are the best practices for the *analysis, evaluation, conclusion,* and *recommendation:*

Analysis is the *gathering* and *verifying* of the *pertinent facts* about the target problem. The facts presented in the story are only those *necessary* to tell the story and are listed in the order that the story is told. The audience must agree that the facts are *pertinent and accurate,* or all that follows will be irrelevant. Facts that are out of sequence or extraneous can confuse and blunt the balance of the story.

Evaluation is the *unbiased* meaning of the facts; it is not an opinion but analytically/empirically derived or from independently validated/respected sources. Evaluation is presented at the level the audience can understand. For example, if you say the sales trend next month is predicted to decline because the Statistical Process Control Index derived by statistical theory is greater than two standard deviations, your message is DOA (unless it is before a statistically savvy group). You must have the audience agree with the evaluation, so a better story to tell is that the sales trend is predicted to go down next month because sales were 50% higher the past two months than the same time last year, and using statistical analysis along with interviews from our key store managers confirms that we cannot expect to maintain this elevated sales level much longer.

The **conclusion and recommendation** should be concise and specific. For recommendations, it also helps to have options, especially when capital/budget is needed. If the costs are relatively small/moderate, include two choices. For larger projects, it is best to have three choices, as people respond to the low cost as cheap, the high as expensive, and the middle as what can be afforded.

Another best practice when preparing a presentation is to ask yourself whether there is content that is unknowable that can take you off point. This is critical to prevent going down a rat-hole. When developing the facts, we tend to use too many; then it often follows that a particular fact triggers an off-topic Q&A or discussions between managers that burn time and add no value.

For example, a presentation listed all the parts of a manufacturer with constrained inventory that affected the associated products to be able to fulfill demand. Instead of simply stating that there were part shortages affecting fulfilling demand, a discussion ensued as to which parts management cared about rather than how part shortages were impacting billings—which brings us to the metrics about knowing your audience.

When speaking to management, you should speak to the lowest level of understanding. Simplicity breeds understanding and saves an executive from the embarrassment of asking a question that may show ignorance. Further, your audience is attentive but not forgiving. Be mindful of three key formulas:

Intelligence = 1 / Title. The higher the level in the organization, the inversely less intelligent they are. Folk at the top have human skills and business savvy, but despite all the press, most are not the sharpest knives in the drawer—after all, that's your job!

Politeness = Title. The higher the level in the organization, the more polite they are—but do not confuse politeness with understanding what you are presenting. For the latter, you must check that they both understand what you said and agree with it.

Forgiveness = 1 / (Title)^2. The higher the level in the organization, the faster, by the inverse square, they will *not* forgive you if you get any fact wrong. This is the most significant point about what to avoid in a presentation. There may be honest disagreement about evaluation, conclusion, and recommendation that will not be faulted, but management expects and demands that you get the facts right.

Finally, a good storyteller presents with good form and format. Even in the modern era of people dressing in blue jeans and sandals, how you look and speak matters. Laugh at the man in a suit and tie, but if he's well dressed and articulate, he elevates his credibility. However, the key to appearance is to know your audience, and presenting to a room of tech geeks is typically done in a T-shirt and flip-flops!

Form and format are important to the presentation, and it is best practice to quantify and, when valuable, to visualize (trends are especially good to visualize). Further, insights tell that which is not known—*but* be sure to express that insight in understandable terms. A complex mathematical term may derail the presentation, as it will be unknown without the requisite mathematical knowledge. Showing management how smart you are is accomplished by talking not above them but to them.

STARTING AN ANALYTICS PROJECT

If data is the gas for your car, then analytics is the engine that creates the movement to transport an organization from a reporting factory to an analytics powerhouse. However, few organizations have succeeded in taking the journey toward making decisions on analytics insights. A framework is needed to move from problem definition to the actual adoption of analytics for decision-making.

The framework to travel through an analytics project has five stages supported by the four components of building an Analytics Culture: Mindset, People, Process, and Systems. These components need to be considered and aligned at each stage of the project to achieve the adoption of analytics as the mechanism for decision-making.

But before starting the analytics journey, many companies need to gain bandwidth to make people's time available. Bandwidth is gained by eliminating unused, little-used, and ineffective reports and automating processes and reporting. As such, we will first outline the process of *eliminate and automate* and then proceed to build the *analytics project framework*.

To ensure success, we have included a section on *looping back and measuring success*. During the analytics project, issues may arise at a stage that becomes a showstopper. At that point, you must *loop back* to a prior stage. When the project is complete, you must quantifiably *measure success* in the business's performance to ensure the ROI, which will stamp the credentials of analytics and enable you to showcase the success to the organization. What follows in this section has been developed by the Finance Analytics Institute and taught at FAI's Analytics Academy.

Eliminate and Automate

Too often, AI and analytics projects are stopped because the executive says there is no budget to hire additional people for analytics. To ensure the availability of the budget by gaining the bandwidth of the existing headcount, we are tackling two issues at once.

Eliminate

The first step to free up bandwidth or money is to *eliminate* unused, little-used, redundant, or low-value reports. Many reports produced by support functions are never opened or little reviewed by the executives, so much so that they waste money, time, and talent and should be stopped immediately.

When sending reports by email, it can be difficult to evaluate whether they are being opened or used by the receiver. But organizations that have advanced their reporting tools beyond Excel and PowerPoint and are using EPM/ERP or data visualization tools have a log describing who opens the reports and when. As such, it is easy to see which reports are **unused** and can be eliminated.

Little-used reports can be similarly detected: they are opened for a very short time. To reduce such irrelevant reporting, a dialogue is needed with the receivers of the reports where the reporting team brings the data log to the conversation.

In many organizations, marketing, operations, finance, and even HR often produce similar reports for executives without aligning who is producing what. **Redundant** reports are also captured from a dialogue with the receivers and should be eliminated.

Low-value reports need to be eliminated too, but when was the last time a report receiver volunteered to get fewer reports? Probably never! If receivers are asked if a report is being used, they will always answer yes. Low-value reports are eliminated by asking the executives if they would rather have the current hindsight information that cannot be used for decision-making or if it should be replaced by a new high-value report providing insight for the receiver's decision-making.

We estimate that 40–70% of the reports currently produced can be eliminated to free up time to elevate reporting with AI-enabled analytics. For example, a finance organization in a major consumer credit company managed to cut regular reports from 1,300 to 600 and eliminated 400 hours in their report production effort. Their approach was simple: (i) assemble a list of all reports, (ii) define how much time is spent on each report, (iii) meet with business stakeholders and define critical reports to keep, and (iv) identify reports that were not used, little used, redundant, or low value.

Automate

The second step to gain more bandwidth and capacity is to *automate* processes and reporting. Within automation of processes, the current new buzzword is *robotic process automate* (RPA), which refers to software that can do basic repetitive tasks across applications, like AR and AP tasks.

Another area is automation for management reporting using tools like EPM, BI, and Data Visualization instead of Excel. As we have identified, Excel reporting wastefully consumes about $60 billion of labor annually. Moving from Excel into reporting and visualization tools reduces the time it takes to make and update regular reporting.

Report automation improves the speed at which a report lands in the hands of a stakeholder and reduces the errors that constantly occur when humans touch large spreadsheet reports. In general, report automation has three large advantages over Excel: automating the pull of data, hands-free report production, and packetizing reports for email or online self-service.

Analytics Project Framework

After having eliminated and automated processes and reports, bandwidth and expense budgets are available to start to *elevate* the organization with analytics. We are now ready to launch the first analytics project, which follows five stages, as depicted in Figure A.10: *Problem Definition*, then *Data*, then *Analytics Insight*, then *Insight to Action*, and finally *Solution Adoption*. Notice that the project follows the underlying arrow of the analytics Roadmap components of Mindset, People, Process, and Systems.

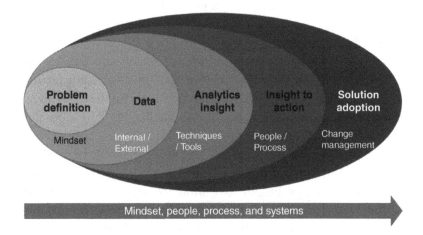

Figure A.10   Analytics project path.

Step 1: Problem Definition

Analytics projects begin to identify a problem to solve by applying analytics tools and techniques to implement the results for better performance.

Often a project delivers a quick result, only to find that it cannot be adopted because it addressed the "wrong" problem. As such, the solution is to become better at asking the right questions up front in order to tackle the right problems from the beginning and not start the journey before the right problem statement has been defined. As Albert Einstein said, "If I had only one hour to save the world, I would spend fifty-five minutes defining the problem, and only five minutes finding the solution."[6]

When defining the problem, the appropriate *Mindset* is needed that advanced analytics can indeed be applied to solve problems. We follow a progression to define the *need* or problem to be solved, then determine the associated *ROI* for solving the problem, then assure the problem is within an *organization* that is receptive to starting an analytics project, and finally develop a *game plan* for the budget and schedule for the project:

Need starts with an understanding of a clear and concise stated problem definition. Do not spend months working with external consultants to define a problem; simply start at a high level by articulating the issue's importance, address the resources needed, and then secure buy-in from executives to move forward from this initial phase.

It is important not to jump to a solution and stay focused on defining the right issue before making an elevator pitch to the executives for their input, feedback, and approval. With approval in hand, the AC is ready to finalize the entire problem definition and present it to the organization.

Do not shy away from solving advanced problems, as this is within the capability of AI-enabled analytics. As we have said several times, an insight that influences decisions and impacts the strategic direction is found using mathematics, not arithmetic. If we just apply arithmetic to provide information, it is not an analytics project but merely improved reporting. An analytics project needs to have an elevation grounded in mathematics to generate insight for data-driven decisions.

ROI is the performance measure used to evaluate the return on investment, which can be used to compare the efficiency of several different investments. When starting an analytics project, there must be an ROI that defines the monetary return of that investment and how that compares to other investments. If the ROI is not at least 10X, reconsider the need. ROI should include investments in both systems and people, as often requisite AI-enabled analytics and the right or sufficient people are lacking.

Organization is the home to start analytics, and it is essential to choose wisely, as some executives are more receptive than others. Even with 10X ROI, many an executive has the attitude that good enough is good enough, meaning budget not spent is costs contained.

The **game plan** is the preparation of a realistic, practical, structured project schedule and budget to move from problem definition to solution adoption. An AC will easily lose credibility if the time and money spent on the analytics project are way over what was approved.

As discussed, the game plan *must* have an executive sponsor if delays happen or additional funding is needed. Another benefit of the executive sponsor is that the AC has a sparring partner to whom to present the project's progression and provide candid feedback and advice throughout the process.

Finally, the project budget must be able to go all the way from start to end without needing additional funds or gaining interim approvals. For example, an analytics project in a Fortune 100 company failed because the AC had only verbal, not written, confirmation from the executive sponsor to complete the project. After successfully completing the first three stages, the project was abruptly ended as the company reprioritized its spending.

Step 2: Data

During the *Problem Definition* stage, the data to be used for the analytics project has been identified. In the *Data* stage, there are two key areas to consider: *collecting data* and *exploration, validation*, and *cleaning data*.

Collecting data: Values from the past and future include *internal data* already available in our own databases (or spreadsheets) or *external data* that can be either acquired or collected for free. But data can also be created: *calculated data* is also, well, data.

Internal data is information, statistics, and trends that a company is discovering in its operations. It includes facts and figures pulled from internal databases, software, customers, or other reports. It is not limited to financial data and includes any data throughout any of the organizations in the company that can be applied to solve the defined problem.

In a Fortune 100 company, the finance department noticed how financial performance was highly correlated with customer satisfaction. While financial performance was the department's own data, customer satisfaction was generated in the marketing department. By combining the sources and understanding the relationship between the data, the finance department was able to tell the business how much financial performance would increase with an improvement in customer satisfaction.

External data comes in various forms, including information about the market, customers, and competitors. The external data can be publicly available (e.g. internet searches, financials, etc.) or private data acquired from third parties (Amazon, Google, etc.). Note that external data has no real relevance until it is compared to internal data to generate insights.

For example, a division of an international materials company noticed that its own performance was highly correlated to its top competitor's performance. It also noticed that the competitor's performance was highly correlated to an external production index. As such, using external data with internal data, this division was able to understand its current performance against its competition and was able to predict its and the competitor's future performance using the projection of the external production index.

Calculated data or created data can be developed from internal and/or external data. These calculated fields do not exist in the raw data but are created from arithmetic or mathematics. For example, using the internal sales pipeline data for a sales stage (e.g. Open, Best Case, Commit) of a deal, a calculation can be made of how many revisions have been made to the stage of the deal over time. This calculated field of the number of revisions doesn't exist in the raw internal sales data.

For example, a technology company discovered that the number of revisions of deals in the pipeline was very explanatory for whether a deal would close in each quarter. Cluster analytics revealed that few revisions as well as many revisions was a bad signal of whether a deal would be sold. The sweet spot was deals with a medium number of revisions. Few revisions indicated the deal was too young, and many revisions indicated instability. In both cases, AI-enabled analytics determined the deal had a low propensity to close.

Exploration, validation, and cleaning data provide the basics to ensure that the data to be used for analytics is suitable and capable of the project at hand. *Exploration* speaks to suitability by understanding the characteristics of the data. This is often gained by using data visualization and segmentation (dimensions) to better understand underlying trends.

Validation regards data quality to ensure accuracy, completeness, and accessibility. Validation includes but is not limited to data type checks (whether data is keyed in as numeric or letters), format check (date vs. number), consistency check (whether all cells that need data have data), and unique identifiers in data (a unique factor or sequence of factors to identify each transaction in the dataset).

Data cleaning is the process where corrupt, incorrect, inaccurate, or irrelevant data, files, and dimensions are detected, corrected, or removed from the dataset. Data cleaning can be performed manually, but tools also exist that can automatically handle the cleansing.

Step 3: Analytics Insights

As we learned in Chapter 5, there is a significant difference between information and insight. Information is generated from arithmetic or data visualization, whereas insight is generated from mathematics.

For example, a Fortune 100 company hired a consultant to help the finance department with an analytics project to move it from just providing information to providing insightful analytics. After spending a quantity of time on steps 1 and 2 in the analytics project framework, the finance department implemented a data visualization tool as the analytics tool. While the tool was useful for data visualization of historical data, it was inappropriate for true analytics to generate insight for executives' data-driven decisions.

To be successful at this stage, organizations need to be able to use advanced analytics like correlations, regression formula, cluster analytics, AI-generated predictions, etc., and AI-enabled analytics tools are the better enabler. Along with the right tools are the right people. So, in short order, *Analytics Insights* boils down to the *People* and *System* components of the Roadmap:

People: Getting the right people means finding those who are curious, capable, and smart, and those with the right aspirations (to ensure long-term employment). An approach when searching for the right talent is for HR to apply advanced analytics! HR is not a function many expect to use analytics, but why not?

Companies rate their employees every year and have data on high, medium, and low performers. They also have information on years of experience, college, career progression, number of jobs changes, etc. Using that information on current employees and applying systematic and artificial intelligence, companies can paint a picture of high-, medium-, and low-profile performers among their current employees. With this insight, the HR recruiter can screen external candidates, too, looking for those who possess similar attributes to the top performers, who should then be brought into the interview process.

Systems: Getting the right tool was discussed in Chapter 7, which identified the elements as *cost-effective, easy to use, speed to value, efficient* to solve the business problem, and analytics *interpretable* by business users.

Most analytics vendors, especially those that are small to medium size, offer free POCs, so there is no excuse for not getting the right tool for the project. Make sure the vendors do not come and showcase visualization tools, as those are mainly for descriptive analysis. It is important that chosen vendors use their tools to find real insight into a company's data by applying AI-enabled analytics.

Another item to consider is outsourcing analytics. This is a new concept where a company can leap into becoming an analytics powerhouse by outsourcing analytics to an internal department or third party that has the people and systems.

Here, a vendor delivers advanced analytics or even consultancy to an organization without the organization having to invest in systems or people. This concept is for the organization that wants to implement analytics without significant up-front investment and is accustomed to a subscription-based solution (e.g. Software as a Service or off-shore Center of Excellence).

Outsourcing is the analytics tool and AC all rolled into one predictive and prescriptive analytics powerhouse utilizing AI to provide unbiased forecasts and insight solutions for data-driven decisions. The cost benefit is significant as it can be delivered for at least two-thirds less cost than the traditional approach of hiring people and acquiring tools. It also delivers the benefits of immediate access to analytics without having to wait for the implementation and training cycles.

The downside to this approach is that it mitigates an organization building an Analytics Culture in-house with its own people, and therefore the analytics journey does not become part of the existing employees' career path. Also, analytics will be provided based on requests and not something any group of people is doing continuously. As such, it is up to the company to evaluate the pros and cons before deciding whether to outsource analytics people and systems or build the Analytics Culture in-house.

Step 4: Insight to Action

After finding the valuable insight from analytics, it needs to be used for data-driven decisions by executives. To make this happen requires *buy-in, speed,* and *storytelling.*

Buy-In is when the insight aligns with the buy-in from the problem definition. If the AC has not followed the game plan and analyzed a different value proposition, trust will be lost immediately.

It might sometimes be tempting to deviate from the game plan when working through the analytics, which is fine, but the main findings need to align with the agreed plan defined in the first step of the analytics project.

Speed: The term *actionable* regarding decision-making means a task that can be accomplished shortly. Insight needs to be provided within enough time to still be relevant for executives. If executives must wait for several weeks or months to get the latest analytics update, insights become irrelevant and obsolete for decision-making.

Storytelling is being able to articulate a clear and concise message when presenting analytics findings to executives. To become a successful storyteller, you must know and understand the audience. As a rule of thumb, the higher the level of the executive, the lower the level of complexity that should be in the presentation. One could say there is an inverse relationship between executive level and analytics complexity when it comes to telling stories with analytics.

Only present what is relevant, as time with executives is limited. Use visuals instead of large tables with hundreds of numbers. But if the executives prefer numbers, present the fewest possible, in tables of limited size.

It is also important to end a presentation with the "how to," meaning how to use the analytics findings in the decision-making process and what decision is recommended for the executives to take. Ending this way gives the AC the opportunity to influence the executive's use of data analytics for decision-making.

Step 5: Solution Adoption

The last phase in an analytics project is to get the solution adopted. While a new solution can be implemented, it does not mean the business will adopt it. Executive commitment and communications will be essential to adoption, as humans naturally resist change. Executives should be at the forefront to communicate why the solution should be adopted and what benefits the stakeholders will get from such a solution.

For example, in an IT cloud business, the VP of Sales was constantly against new initiatives, as he was "the one who knows the business the best" and thereby the one understanding which deals to have in the pipeline forecast. Nevertheless, the VP's manager, the SVP of the business, decided to launch an analytics project with the Finance organization. After two months, a solution was ready to be implemented to help the VP of Sales determine which deals in the pipeline for a given quarter had the highest probability of closing. Naturally, the VP of Sales was against using analytics to run his organization; but after understanding the benefits, the VP's mind was changed. Being able to describe the "why" and the benefits increases the likelihood that a solution will be adopted.

Solutions are always easier to get adopted if they mirror the culture of a company. If a company is run such that "good enough is good enough," and decisions are made based on gut feeling rather than analytics, it is hard to change the organization to start including advanced technologies in the decision-making process. Also, if an organization has a culture of high transparency and collaboration, the solution should align to that style, and the AC will have to provide a significant amount of feedback to all stakeholders throughout the entire analytics project.

Finally, it is vital to *burn the bridges*, meaning after launching the analytics project, the company must start to make decisions based on analytics and does not go back to making decisions based on gut feeling and single case examples as in the past.

Loop Back and Measure Success

Two elements are critical for an analytics project to become and remain a success. First is the *loop-back* mechanism when moving through the five project stages, which may not be a one-way street. While the stages move from left to right, if a project is failing in one of the stages, it may need to loop back to a previous stage to redefine the scope or resolve the issue. As an example, if stage 3, *Analytics Insight*, is not possible because relevant insight from the data cannot be gained, there is a need to loop back to the *Data* stage to learn if additional or new data is available. If that is not the case, then there may be a need to loop back to the *Problem Definition* stage to redefine the project's scope. The second element is to *measure the success* of the project, meaning the organization needs to quantify that the solution delivers what was intended.

A project that is properly managed and supported by the sponsoring executive has a high probability of achieving measurable success. However, change, no matter how beneficial, is often fraught with peril, and the analytics project can face "death" through the misalignment of any of the four components of the Roadmap to implementing an Analytics Culture of data-driven decisions (Mindset, People, Process, and Systems). Figure A.11 depicts the "pathways of death."

In the first stage, *Problem Definition*, an analytics project can be abandoned due to Death by Mindset: executives or business stakeholders are not aligned with the AC about the real problem that needs to be solved or if there is any problem that needs to be solved.

The major challenge in the *Data* stage is whether the right data is available and if the quality of the data is sufficient for running an ana-

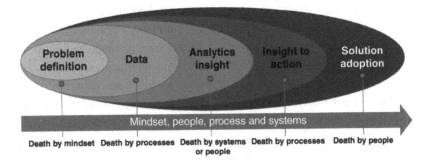

Figure A.11 Pathways of death.

lytics project. Data Governance (described in Chapter 5) is an essential process and why Death by Process often occurs in this stage. Ensuring that the data used in decisions is accurate, complete, timely, and accessible is the foundation for the next three steps. If data does not satisfy these few criteria, then the solution output can only be as good as the data input—garbage in, garbage out!

To get successfully through the *Analytics Insight* stage, investments in either systems and/or people are often needed. Death by Systems becomes a reality where there is no money to invest in AI-enabled analytics tools or if an investment is being made in the wrong tool: for example, when a data visualization tool is conflated as an analytics tool. As we have learned throughout the book, visualization tools cannot often be used to find the insight for data-driven decisions, only information about what has happened in the data.

The people challenge arises when no money is allocated to hire the right candidates or if internal talents are not trained to produce analytics insights. In both cases, Death by People is the outcome, as no analytics insight will be gained without getting the right people on board.

Sometimes the project advances all the way to stage 4, *Insight to Action*, and then dies. If there is no buy-in from stakeholders to use the analytics in decision-making, another Death by Process occurs. In this case, death is due to the lack of a Decision Governance process (described in Chapter 5) that identifies the decision-making participants, steps, and authorities. If these steps are not well-defined, decisions will not be made based on analytics findings.

In the *Solution Adoption* stage, Death by People happens when people are unwilling to advance their capabilities to understand what the analytics findings mean, or stakeholders have a negative attitude toward adopting reporting from new tools and techniques. Here, people cling to the old ways of doing what has always been done.

To get the analytics project successfully completed from start to finish, the AC must be attentive and always attuned to ensuring that these modes of failure are exorcised as soon as they become visible—and, even better, anticipating how these might arise and proactively preventing them.

EPILOGUE

With the first successful analytics project in hand, attention can turn to propagating the Analytics Culture by scaling analytics and "crossing the chasm." Success breeds success, but the derailments that could affect the first project still lurk as you proceed to the next analytics project. Over time, these issues will lessen in strength and frequency, but vigilance will always be required.

When considering scaling analytics, keep the following considerations in mind. (i) Should there be an Analytics Group in the company, and is it central or decentral within the organization? (ii) What is the appropriate level and source of funding (i.e. allocated budget or self-funded)? (iii) How many additional ACs are needed, and when is the required timetable to assign them? (iv) What analytics tools, training, and additional people are needed to effectively complete subsequent projects? And (v) what and how much outside consulting resources are needed to complete the transformation process and attain self-sufficiency?

These are exciting times as we stand at the vanguard of the brave new world of AI and analytics. What we do now will be transformative to business performance. Those who look at the future and see risk in adopting analytics will become extinct, as nature applies her laws of survival of the fittest. Those who enthusiastically see and embrace the endless possibilities in the future with AI will be rewarded. As we have stated throughout this book, the journey to AI-enabled analytics is not long, difficult, or expensive—it is disciplined!

The authors wish you smooth sailing on your AI and analytics voyage—may the wind be at your back!

NOTES

1. Sorensen, J.H. and Zwerling, R.J. (2020. Analytics business partnering (part 4 of 7), strategic leadership. LinkedIn. https://www.linkedin.com/pulse/analytics -business-partnering-part-4-7-strategic-hybholt-sorensen.
2. BrainyQuote. (n.d.). Normal Schwarzkopf quotes. https://www.brainyquote.com/ quotes/norman_schwarzkopf.
3. Kotter, J.P. and Cohen, D. (2013). *The Heart of Change: Real-Life Stories of How People Change Their Organizations*, 1. Harvard Business Press.
4. Goodreads. (n.d.). Mark Twain quote. https://www.goodreads.com/quotes/21422- i-didn-t-have-time-to-write-a-short-letter-so.
5. Gadiesh, O. and Gilbert, J.I. (2001). Transforming corner-office strategy into front-line action. *Harvard Business Review Magazine*.
6. Quote Investigator. (n.d.). https://quoteinvestigator.com/2014/05/22/solve.

About the Authors

LAWRENCE S. MAISEL

Lawrence S. Maisel is president of DecisionVu, a management consultancy specializing in performance management, data analytics, operations improvements, and IT business management. He is an experienced senior executive with a demonstrated track record of success and proven leadership skills and expertise to drive efficiency and control through improving financial and performance management practices including planning and analysis, AI-enabled business and data analytics, cost analysis, and operating process redesign.

He has extensive industry experiences with diverse and various-sized organizations including industrial and bio-pharmaceutical, financial services and insurance, and media companies. An excellent communicator and team player possessing skills that enables him to collaborate with colleagues at all organizational levels, he has managed Six Sigma and change-management programs from launch to successful conclusion.

He has held senior management positions as COO, CFO, controller, and vice president FP&A. He is a former senior partner at KPMG Consulting, leading, globally, its Strategy and Performance Management consulting practice; and vice president of business strategy at Oracle, with responsibilities for designing and marketing the company's financial management and enterprise performance management (EPM) systems.

Mr. Maisel is a hands-on consultant with proven leadership skills, sound strategic thinking, and deep financial expertise to drive efficiency and control, with numerous experiences in redesigning and implementing process capabilities resulting in improved business processes and operations, lower service costs, and increased service levels. He has a track record of managing diverse projects and teams.

He is a CPA, MBA, and CGMA and received AICPA's "Thought Leader award for creating and operating its Center for Excellence in Financial Management." He has authored *Predictive Business Analytics: Forward-looking Capabilities to Improve Business Performance* (John Wiley & Sons), co-created with Drs. Kaplan and Norton the Balanced Scorecard approach, authored *Performance Management: The Balanced Scorecard Approach*, and co-authored with Drs. Kaplan and Cooper *Implementing Activity-Based Cost Management: Moving from Analysis to Action*.

He is a former adjunct professor at Columbia University's Graduate School of Business, where he developed and taught a graduate course (MBA program) focused on the principles and practices of designing, evaluating, and using strategic management in today's organizations to achieve performance excellence and increase shareholder value by executing strategies.

Mr. Maisel is a member of the advisory board of Aurora Predictions; is a senior advisor, University of Pennsylvania, Wharton Business School; and served on advisory boards for Forrester Research, Gartner, Apptio, and IBM. He has been a keynote speaker at numerous professional conferences, lead presenter on numerous webinars; and developed and led training courses on business and data analytics for the Association of Financial Professionals (AFP) and Finance Analytics Institute.

ROBERT J. ZWERLING

Robert James Zwerling is a high-tech serial entrepreneur with 30 years experience of founding and growing software companies across telecommunication, manufacturing, distribution, high data availability, predictive analytics, and artificial intelligence. He is an accomplished business leader, speaker, and author on predictive analytics, creator of Systematic Intelligence™ that enables intelligent analytics data mining, inventor of the innovative One-Touch AI forecast with no need for model training, and designer of the Systematic Thinking™ methodology for the application of AI and analytics to solve business problems.

Mr. Zwerling is at the vanguard of business digital transformation and considered a thought leader in analytics and novel strategist in the deployment of AI. He has been a keynote speaker on AI and delivered highly rated lectures and courses attended by analysts, managers, and executives throughout North America, Middle East, and Europe. Along with Jesper H. Sorensen, Mr. Zwerling has coauthored numerous articles and research papers in AI and analytics and the groundbreaking book *Implementing an Analytics Culture for Data Driven Decisions*.

Mr. Zwerling is founder and managing director of Aurora Predictions, providing AI-enabled analytics software with its intuitive/ no-code interface and no need for data science or programming skills, which automatically delivers AI insights that move the business's needle. Aurora LightZ™ snaps on to sales, finance, and operations data and spreadsheets to provide deep-dive insights with AI forecasting and predictive analytics that is fast to value to reveal unknown risks and unseen opportunities in businesses ranging from $10 million to $40 billion across sales, finance, operations, supply chain, demand planning, and inventory organizations.

He is co-founder, with Jesper H. Sorensen, of the Finance Analytics Institute, which teaches how to implement analytics through articles, research papers, surveys, benchmarks, and the Analytics Academy. FAI publishes "Temperature of Finance," an annual global survey of the state of analytics in the finance organization; the Analytics Benchmark Survey, the first quantitative measure of the position and progress of an individual and business on the Roadmap to an Analytics Culture; and the Analytics Academy, which brings vision, voice, and clarity to the value of analytics and the Roadmap to implement a culture of data driven decisions.

Mr. Zwerling's career spans leadership and executive positions at Fortune 500 companies in power generation and high-tech. As founder and CEO of multiple software companies, he managed global growth and exits to a major public company DXC Technology Company (NYSE:DXC), a foreign public company, and a private party.

He has a Bachelor of Engineering (magna cum laude) in mechanical engineering from Stony Brook University and a Master of Science in mechanical engineering (major in thermodynamics and fluid mechanics) from CSU Los Angeles. He is a member of the Tau Beta

Pi engineering honor society and a licensed professional engineer, mechanical engineering, in California.

JESPER H. SORENSEN

Jesper Hybholt Sorensen is a result-oriented and innovative finance executive with extensive experience leading large global finance teams for multi-billion-dollar businesses. He has a proven track record of advancing the analytics agenda in Fortune 100 companies. By applying advanced analytics and strategic leadership, he influences executives to make data-driven decisions and has received several rewards and recognition for improving top-line growth and profitability from this mindset.

Mr. Sorensen is currently a vice president of finance at Oracle and has a background with large corporations like IBM and DuPont where he has been a controller and head of finance. Throughout his career, he has led large company-wide finance transformation projects; and with his recognized framework of building the right skillset and toolbox, he has enabled finance professionals to influence business decisions and set the strategic direction for the company.

Together with Robert J. Zwerling, he is the co-founder of the Finance Analytics Institute, an educational platform bringing books, articles, research, benchmarking, and its Analytics Academy to help business professionals explore data in a new way to discover insights and foresight to unlock the endless potential. He also co-authored the book *Implementing an Analytics Culture for Data Driven Decisions: A Manifesto for Next Generation Finance* with Robert J. Zwerling.

Mr. Sorensen holds several advisory positions including advisory board member for Aurora Predictions and advisory board member for Born Capital, a venture capital firm investing in startups in the CFO-Tech space. As an advisor, he guides business executives on industry benchmarks, how to apply analytics in different business scenarios, and how to optimize analytics software to enable better decision-making.

He is a Next Generation Finance thought leader, dedicated to helping the global finance community advance their capabilities and enabling them to implement an Analytics Culture into their business partnering approach. As such, he is a highly respected conference keynote speaker and academy lecturer who is featured at several events each year worldwide covering topics like strategic business partnering, the modern CFO, and applied advanced analytics.

He holds a Master in Economics and Business Management and a Bachelor in Economics, both from the University of Aarhus in Denmark. He is a certified Six Sigma Green Belt and is certified in risk management and strategic decision-making from Stanford University.

About the Website

$500 billion is spent annually by IT on enterprise software for every aspect of business operations—yet significant forecast errors, supply-chain disconnects, excess discounts, stock-outs, sales deals that don't close on time, and so on cost business $242 billion annually in under-optimized planning and excess labor; because state-of-the-art enterprise software and associated reporting from BI, data visualization, and spreadsheets speak largely to the past of "what happened" and "where it happened." The critical questions about the future needed for better planning of "what will happen" and "how to make the future happen" can only be answered by AI-enabled analytics. But analytics and AI tools are typically complex, need high-quality data, and are designed for the data scientist and mathematician. Enter Aurora Predictions' LightZ™ software, to enable the business users with an intuitive/no-code environment that automatically applies AI and analytics to finance, sales, and operations data to get fast-to-value forecasts, predictions, correlations, and insights that move the business's needle. Simply load data from spreadsheets, and with no need for model training or data science/statistics skills, LightZ will reveal unseen risks and unknown opportunities for data-driven decisions that lead to better planning and increase business performance. Use LightZ to automate existing spreadsheet reports and gain the application of analytics on the data; or connect LightZ with BI, data warehouse, or transactional data to enable better budgets, forecasts, S&OP, revenue quality management, product portfolio management, sales deal prediction closings, cost optimization, and much more.

To register for the Free Version of LightZ™, visit https://aurorapredictions.com/aurora-lightz-4all/#Form.

Index